Threats of Revolution in Britain
1789–1848

Threats of Revolution in Britain 1789–1848

MALCOLM I. THOMIS
and
PETER HOLT

First published 1977 by
THE MACMILLAN PRESS LTD
London and Basingstoke
Associated companies in New York Dublin
Melbourne Johannesburg and Madras

ISBN 0 333 21374 2 (hard cover)
0 333 21375 0 (paper cover)

Printed in Great Britain at the
University Press, Cambridge

To Jackie and Lydia

Contents

Acknowledgements   viii

Note on References   viii

   Introduction   1
1 The Jacobin Threat   5
2 Luddites, Hampden Clubs and the Pentrich Rebels   29
3 The Union Societies, Peterloo and the Scottish Radicals   62
4 The Reform of Parliament: The Middle-class Threat   85
5 Chartism: The Working-class Threat   100
6 Prospects of Revolutionary Success 1789–1848   117

Select Bibliography and Works Cited   135

Index   141

Acknowledgements

Our thanks are due to the staff of the libraries and record offices of England and Scotland who helped us with the material cited in the Bibliography, and to our typists, Peggy Burke, Margaret Hendry and Lydia Holt.

Note on References

References in square brackets within the text relate to material itemised in the Select Bibliography and Works Cited section (pages 135–9), which is divided into Primary and Secondary sources, with P and S as the prefix-indicators for the type of material referred to. Page-numbers are italicised. For example: [P6] and [S10, *162*].

COVER ILLUSTRATION: George Cruikshank's print (9 March 1820) – '*The Cato Street Conspirators*, on the Memorable Night of the 23rd of Feby 1820 at the Moment when Smithers the Police Officer was stabbed; NB The Scene faithfully represented from the Description of Mr Ruthven. The View of the Interrior correctly Sketched on the Spot.'

Introduction

This study has no pretensions to being an exhaustive examination of the subject. It is more of an exploratory investigation of a theme which has interested most historians of the period a little, but not sufficiently to deflect them from their main pursuits. The material, both primary and secondary, which any authoritative work would need to embrace is enormous; here the material is only sampled, and students are directed to some of the best-known secondary texts which have touched upon the issues raised in this one. At the same time an attempt has been made to give coherence to a wide range of movements, a few of which have been examined in some detail for illustrations of general propositions concerning the threat of revolution in these years.

It would be exaggerating the strength, importance and continuity of the theme to suggest that this is a study of the revolutionary movement in British politics during the period 1789–1848. There is no precise revolutionary movement to trace, but there is an idea of revolution, elusive in its location in time and space, elusive above all in its shape and form, and this idea must perhaps be approached obliquely from several different angles.

It can be approached primarily through a study of the political movement which drew inspiration from the American and French Revolutions. To call this a movement for parliamentary reform would be too narrowing and too restricting, for it was concerned with political rights in the abstract as well as in their realisation through the particular machinery that Britain had developed. It did, however, tend to focus upon the issue of parliamentary reform, which is central to the period, and even this manifestation was often frightening to its observers. Historians do not, on the whole, confuse the reform movement with a revolutionary one, but they are capable of seeing how it might have been so confused, how indeed it was so confused, by many contemporaries. The political reformers produced through this period both an ideology and an organisation which were revolutionary for their time and which might have been turned in the direction of political revolution. Their movement was invariably open to misinterpretation, unintentional or deliberate, and it was always likely to attract to its fringes people who were prepared to advocate direct methods of political action. The political reform movement was the starting-point of most of the revolutionary conspiracies of the period and as such must feature prominently in this analysis.

A second contributing element to the growth and strength of the idea of revolution was the attitude of successive governments and the policies which they chose to adopt. It was the government that was chiefly responsible for confusing reform with revolution and reading revolution into many a situation where it did not exist. And the result of this confusion and the inexpendient policies that flowed from it was often the creation of revolutionaries where none had previously been. Sometimes by mistaken policies of repression, where the menace was largely imaginary, sometimes by deliberate provocation of confrontation where violence could have been avoided, governments helped to create and sustain that very danger to themselves that they supposedly wished to avoid. The activities of governments made no small contribution to the development of the idea of revolution, which was disseminated and given hard form in large measure through the agency of an institution committed to its elimination.

The hard form is to be seen in the series of conspiracies which threatened to remove revolution from the realms of theory and translate it to the world of practical politics. They are scattered throughout this period, and their instigators envisaged the overthrow of the government by revolutionary coup in the capital, uprisings in the provinces, or with the help of foreign intervention. But whichever plan they embraced they had the common characteristic of being small minorities who never came near to having the mass support necessary for success. Revolutionary plans reached a large audience only through the campaigns of the parliamentary reformers in 1832 and the threats of the Chartists later, who openly threatened the government with revolution as an attempted means of coercion: but this was revolution as tactical talk.

If revolution never became a popular cause, it is necessary to inquire if the period's popular movements ever had the potential of becoming revolutionary. Popular discontent traditionally found expression in food-rioting and might, when associated with a political cause, assume alarming proportions, as in the case of the Gordon Riots of 1780. The years of the French Revolution and the subsequent wars witnessed more appearances of Church/King riots, which the authorities were ready enough to encourage, and militia riots, naval mutinies, and extensive food-riots, which were much less acceptable manifestations of discontent. The economic and social changes associated with industrialisation added a further range of grievances which produced popular protest and the potential for mass involvement in revolutionary action if the working classes could be mobilised for revolutionary purposes. Luddism was a popular movement with minimal political content. Chartism, a quarter of a century later, was a popular movement of social protest which took a highly politicised form; but neither was a popular revolutionary movement.

This book traces these interconnected themes of political reform, government hostility, conspiracy and popular movements over the period 1789–1848, and in so doing attempts to give clearer identity to the idea of revolution within British politics and society of these years, to assess its strength, and to explain its failure.

1   The Jacobin Threat

The British Jacobins of the late eighteenth century derived their name from revolutionary France, but their political role had little in common with that of their French examples. Their name was a blanket term of abuse such as societies find it convenient to employ to cover all those who disturb their complacency and settled ways of thought with ideas involving radical change. And just as contemporaries found it convenient to label as Jacobins all reformers of various kinds, however remote from the power and fury of the Frenchmen, so have historians been content to use this easily accessible if misleading name for Britons who never came close to leading a revolution in their own country. [s67, *14*]

The ideology of the British reformers was a curious mixture of the old and the new. To counter the charge that they were merely unpatriotic importers of French ideas they appealed to British history as their justification and found their heroes in John Hampden of Ship Money fame or the makers of the Glorious Revolution of 1688, rather than in the demagogues of the Paris streets or the National Assembly. They talked of restoration rather than innovation, of popular rights in Saxon times which Joseph Gerrald, a London Corresponding Society delegate to the British Convention, offered his jurors as a defence of current attempts 'to petition parliament for the restoration of the right of universal suffrage'. [p6] Parliament, Thomas Muir told the Convention, was to be 'restored to its original purity', which had been lost somewhere in time as a result of the Norman Conquest, King John, the Tudor monarchs, or those who had undermined the Revolution Settlement of 1689. [s35, *109, 249–50*] The reformers of the 1790s talked not of an impending revolution but rather of a previous revolution betrayed, and to support their idea of a sovereign people they cited Magna Carta, the Declaration of Arbroath, or the Bill of Rights. In their search for legitimisation the reformers were, of course, dealing in folklore. The solicitor-general told them that universal suffrage had no precedent in the past and that they were appealing to a myth when they talked of

Saxon democracy. [P6] Yet the appeal to the past would long remain part of the reformers' case and indicates a persisting wish to present radical demands as part of a British tradition rather than ideas emanating from contemporary France. Nor can it be assumed that this was mere calculation on the part of the reformers.

The debate was only partly concerned with the distant past for ideas of traditional popular rights were supplemented by more modern notions of the rights of man proclaimed in the American revolt, the writings of Tom Paine and the French Revolution. Appeals to the past were also mingled with appeals to reason and utility in an argument containing a strong element of paradox and internal contradiction. While the reformers as a whole sought respectability for their cause by stressing its ancient lineage, James Mackintosh asserted in 1791 that government 'may be made to be respected, not because it is ancient, or because it is sacred, not because it has been established by Barons, or applauded by Priests, but because it is useful'. [s11, *162*] Tom Paine was foremost among those who stressed reason rather than tradition. He looked to the past only to demonstrate that the British monarchy had been imposed by conquest and maintained by force, without the consent of the people. From his observations of America and France he proclaimed that hereditary government, by its very nature a tyranny, was on the decline, that the mass of the people were entering politics as a potent force, and that popular sovereignty was being established abroad which Britain too should accept, by reason and accommodation rather than unnecessary convulsion. [P51]

Neither the recovery of the Englishman's lost rights nor the achievement of his more recently revealed ones was generally supposed to require revolutionary action, for the political system was open enough to permit the traditional means of public meeting and petitioning to take effect; and even the idea of a people's convention, favoured by the Paineites, was said to be no more than an extension of the mechanism used to get rid of James II by history's most respectable revolutionaries ever. [s11, *197*] Yet whatever means were to be employed for its implementation, the idea of one-man one-vote was, within the context of a privileged, property-based government of the 1790s, a revolutionary one. Having seen the propertied classes demolish the Stuart claims to rule by divine right, the radical reformers were now challenging the divine right of property to serve as the only legitimate basis of government and the right of property-owners to grant or withhold the right to vote. In asserting the right of men, as men, to possess the vote, they were rejecting government by a propertied élite and seeking to replace it by a sovereign people. And this was a revolutionary intent, whatever the means proposed for its accomplishment. To deny that government possessed legitimacy because it was not based upon the consent of the whole people and to envisage those far-reaching changes in the relationship of power and property implied by the demand for one-man one-vote was to reject the whole basis of the existing system and to make accommodation within it totally impossible at this time.

What made this rejection particularly alarming to those in government was the further idea of 'the right to resist power when abused'. This was another relic from the past, a renewal of the old cry of 'justified rebellion', raised in 1688 and given blessing in the philosophies of John Locke. In 1789 Dr Richard Price connected the 'right to resistance' with 'the right to liberty of conscience in religious matters' and the right 'to choose our own governors; to cashier them for misconduct; and to frame a government for ourselves'. [s13, *39, 54*] Cartwright and the Society for the Promotion of Constitutional Information spoke of the right of resistance to oppression. In 1792 the London Corresponding Society proclaimed the people's natural and inalienable rights of resistance to oppression, and of sharing in the government of their country, while John Baxter, one of its members, defended the abstract right of forcible resistance in his pamphlet 'Resistance to Oppression' in 1795. [s5, *71*; s11, *32–3, 312*] Such ideas would be taken up again by Cobbett in later years and by individuals who committed themselves to armed revolt in the post-war period. In the meantime this theoretical justification for rebellion was little more than empty rhetoric in the circumstances of the day. There was little attempt in the 1790s to clarify how far resistance should or would be extended and little sign of its being removed from the realm of theory into that of practical politics.

Reform ideology of the 1790s was not then consciously revolutionary. Some of its principal parts were clearly derived from the nation's past, which allowed their proponents to place themselves within a tradition of reform that was almost conservative. At the same time reform ideology had a number of revolutionary implications, particularly in the claims made for political rights for all men irrespective of their property and in the threats that it extended to those adjudged to have abused the power that they had exercised. The ideology of the reformers possessed an ambiguity that made it moderate and reasonable to those who expounded it, but terrifying and revolutionary to those against whom it was directed.

Yet never in the 1790s did reform threaten to become a mass movement. The labouring poor largely accepted unquestioningly the government and institutions of the country and remained uninvolved in reform demands. Despite the clarity of Paine's language and the wide circulation of his writings among the working population, there remained a vast task of education to be undertaken before the mass of the people would be ready to take part in the reform struggle. In neither England nor Scotland did a mass membership develop for the reform societies. The Friends of the People in England were aristocratic Whigs and their supporters, who favoured moderate reform and who operated from a parliamentary base. Their 'Jacobinism' was evident only to their most hostile foes. The true bearers of the democratic banner were the artisan members of the London Corresponding Society and their allied organisations of the provincial towns such as Norwich, Sheffield, or Nottingham, which were made up of a working-class élite of craftsmen and tradesmen. By contrast the Scottish Friends of the People began as a mixture of Whig aristocrats, gentry and artisans. The meeting that drafted the principles of the Scottish Friends included a painter, tobacconist, printer, stockingmaker, teacher and haberdasher, alongside Presbyterian ministers, a captain, a colonel, and several lords. Weavers, shoemakers and shopkeepers made up much of the membership, and at the Scots' second Convention in Edinburgh, in April 1793, Lord Daer and several advocates presided over a gathering of representatives from thirty-five towns and villages of the manufacturing areas around Glasgow, Edinburgh and Dundee. [s35, 92–3, 105–6; s34, 122] Scotland seems paradoxically to have had both a stronger patrician and a more genuine working-class membership than the London Corresponding Society, with which it formed regular links and which it closely resembled in organisation and its demands for manhood suffrage and annual parliaments. In England, the so-called 'alliance of the industrious', artisans and tradesmen, shopkeepers and small masters, drew upon social groups to whom industrialisation had as yet given no clearly prescribed role, but who would eventually find themselves some little distance above the working masses. [s67, 62] But in neither England nor Scotland were members of the popular societies ever more than a small minority of the population. A contemporary suggestion that the Scottish membership of the Friends of the People reached 67,000 was surely a wild exaggeration; modern estimates of the London Corresponding Society suggest that at its peak it probably had about ten thousand nominal members, of whom perhaps half paid subscriptions. [s34, 122; s56, 169]

In terms of the numbers and kinds of people now actively interested in radical politics the first half of the 1790s was startlingly different from any preceding period, and had these people been intent on re-enacting the French Revolution within Britain the government would have had a serious problem on its hands. But they were not. The London Corresponding Society – the most important organisation of its kind – was a political discussion club that sought to promote reform ideas among working men and to develop contacts and correspondence with similar societies throughout the provinces. A typically earnest group of this kind were the Friends of Liberty at Dundee, with whom the Rev. Thomas Palmer became involved to his great cost. He was a Unitarian minister, and was part of the planned exodus of dissenters to the United States during the persecutions by Church/King mobs. Prior to his departure he was invited by a small group of Dundee weavers to attend their meetings, where he helped them in the writing of their address, which enumerated their many grievances. 'The Friends go on here', he reported, 'with some degree of spirit, they have introduced the practice of reading letters, extracts, and small pamphlets, and then enforcing them by argument, which seems to be likely to produce much good.' [P6] And groups of this kind doubtless existed throughout most of the principal towns and manufacturing centres of the country. The London Corresponding Society was the precursor of many future organisations among working men that would attempt to educate their members at the same time as mobilising them for political protest. Its deliberations were open and its methods too eschewed secrecy, for there could be no popular conversion of opinion without publicity. Petitions, pamphlets and the press were all traditional means of political campaigning, and even their advocacy of conventions was given a traditional setting. A London Corresponding Society delegate to the British Convention in Edinburgh in November 1793, Joseph Gerrald, sought precedents in the Anglo-Saxon 'Folkmote' assemblies, and Charles James Fox drew parallels with the anti-James II assembly of 1688. [P6; s11, *197*]

The artisan reformers, as opposed to the parliamentary Whigs such as Fox and Grey, were compelled to rely on extra-parliamentary agitation and accepted Paine's argument that 'the constitutional method (of gaining reform) would be by a general convention elected for the purpose'. [P51] Events in France, however, made the British government unwilling to tolerate the rise of a British convention, with all its revolutionary implications, however peaceful the declared intent of its advocates. In December 1792 representatives from eighty Scottish reform societies assembled in the city of Edinburgh at the Convention and demanded universal suffrage and annual parliaments. When a young advocate, Thomas Muir, who was prominent in the Friends of the

People in the Glasgow area, suggested that the Convention should accept an Address from the Society of United Irishmen in Dublin and make its stance republican and nationalist, the Convention refused his lead and stressed that its aims were a peaceful reform of Westminster. [s11, *128*; s35, *108*; p6]

Scotland continued to take the initiative over the summoning of popular assemblies and throughout October 1793 William Skirving of Kirkcaldy, secretary to the reconvened Convention due to meet in November, was in contact with Thomas Hardy and the London Corresponding Society. Advocates of one-man one-vote on both sides of the Border were proposing an Anglo-Scottish show of solidarity, protest and defiance following the sentences of transportation recently handed down to Muir and Palmer and the government's rejection of their numerous petitions earlier in the year. Despite predictions that further sacrificial victims would be sought from the reformers' ranks, Joseph Gerrald and Maurice Margarot, on behalf of the London Corresponding Society, attended the Convention, which opened in Edinburgh on 19 November, only four days after the convict ship carrying Muir and Palmer had set sail for Australia. [p6; p9] The Convention reaffirmed its demands for universal suffrage and called for petitions to be signed 'by a number so respectable as to command attention; and it will soon have that respectability, if we have reason on our side'. [p6] The demands were familiar, the means proposed for their achievement respectable enough, but they were being voiced within a framework that deliberately imitated the French revolutionary assembly. The minutes of the Edinburgh gathering opened with: 'First year of the British Convention, one and indivisible' and ended 'ça ira'. They expressed the Convention's 'ardent desire to cultivate a more close union with the societies in England', and there were suggestions for a further Convention to be held in England under the aegis of the London Corresponding Society and the Scottish Friends of the People. But, facing up to the possibilities, members resolved that if the government passed an Act against Conventions, or, if the French invaded, the 'British Convention' should meet secretly as a 'Convention of emergency'. [p6] Beyond touching on the possibility of having to go underground if so forced, the Convention revealed no inclination to set up anything resembling a rival authority to that of parliament or to contemplate plans for an armed revolt. When ordered to disperse by the Lord Provost of Edinburgh, members left peacefully without resistance, and Gerrald, Skirving, and Margarot submitted passively to arrest, which was to lead to transportation sentences of fourteen years for each of them. [p6] Intimidated by this, the Scottish clubs began to disintegrate.

The reformers of this period were confronted by the same dilemma that was to face the Chartists more than forty years later. What they believed to be legitimate demands attainable within the existing framework of politics and society were seen by their opponents as revolutionary ideas that would destroy the existing system. The reformers denied revolutionary intent and they eschewed revolutionary means, believing that what they sought could and would be achieved by an agitation of public opinion and should not be sought by force of arms. But when popularly voiced demands are ignored and Conventions dispersed, reform movements must disintegrate unless they are prepared to escalate their protest by more direct means. Christopher Wyvill, the old leader of the Yorkshire Movement, who had mobilised county associations in favour of moderate reform in 1779–80, rejected the possibility of radical reform by peaceful means in the new situation of the 1790s. 'Many there are,' he wrote to Major Cartwright, already a veteran campaigner for more radical proposals, 'and I am myself of that number, who think a Reform on this principle of Universal Suffrage could not be effected without a Civil War.' [s11, *149–50*] A few reformers probably shared that view and accepted that their agitation would and should lead to revolution and the dawn of a new age; but those who attended the British Convention showed no inclination to convert their assembly for revising public opinion into a centre for armed revolt. And when faced later with the alternatives of silence and inactivity on the one hand, or underground campaigning on the other, scarcely any chose the latter option.

Of the Scottish leaders, Thomas Muir was probably the closest to being a potential revolutionary leader. He stood out among his fellow reformers because of his ardent eloquence, his republican sympathies, his nationalism, his pride at membership of the United Irishmen and his visits to Ireland and France in 1793. But he had no armed organisation behind him, no 'thousands of bearded men in arms' whom he once described as being necessary for successful rebellion, and the Convention of 1792 had rejected the policies he had advocated. [p6] These things were ignored as the government moved against him. His republican sympathies and his agitation of the 'common people's' minds were sufficient to send him to Botany Bay.

In England, Thomas Hardy was the test case of the treasonable intent of the London Corresponding Society, and his trial revealed him as the key organiser within the society, a careful administrator not given to outbursts of passion in speech or in his writing. The prosecution failed to link him with any armed organisation, despite the magnification applied to his personal set of clasp knives and advice given to men seeking to protect themselves from 'anti-Jacobin' riots. If certain individuals, or even certain groups, possessed arms this was no proof of armed conspiracy, and Hardy and his Corresponding Society could not be implicated. Nor could the Crown adduce any convincing evidence that the Conventions in Edinburgh or the talk of a further one to be convened in England had been linked to armed plots. Evidence at Hardy's, as at the Scottish trials, proved only that the Conventions were to be used to agitate public opinion. Hardy had written to Skirving: 'Our petition has been rejected; our minds therefore must be turned to some other plan and more effectual means.' In this context Conventions were to be an extension of peaceful pressure for reform, and only when such peaceful agitation was rejected or reversed did a tiny minority go underground to talk of armed revolt. Hardy and the leaders of reform societies in England and Scotland had no plans for, or connection with, armed revolt and could not be shown to have any such plans. Muir stood apart – as a republican with French and Irish links and later involvement in plans for a French invasion of Scotland. Hardy, after nine days of trial, stood acquitted on the charge of high treason, and the verdicts on his fellow English prisoners were the same. [s7, *128-9*, *140-1*, *147-9*; p6; p19]

It is easy enough, from a distance, to criticise those who, whether from sheer confusion or a wish for political self-preservation, were unable or unwilling to distinguish between reformers and revolutionaries. In the context of the times confusion at least is understandable, if not perhaps excusable, and political survival is a common enough basic aim of all who exercise power. On April Fools' Day 1794 an anonymous placard promised a 'new and entertaining Farce, called La Guillotine or George's Head in the Basket', a show that was 'to conclude with a grand decapitation of Placemen, Pensioners, and German Leeches'. [s11, *285-6*] It was the language of satire rather than the declared intent of revolutionary leaders, yet allegory and neighbouring reality too closely resembled each other for the jest to be comfortably received.

In government eyes, open-air meetings demanding parliamentary reform were both a threat to the established political order and the precursors of revolutionary mobs demanding blood, whatever the protestations of the reformers about the limits of their aims and the means which they would employ to achieve them. The events that had occurred in France from 1789, the coming of war in 1793, and the subsequent invasion scares all combined to ensure that the British government would react in a less than rational manner when confronted with reform demands. The radical nature of the pleas for universal suffrage and their attendant ideas of the rights of man and the sovereignty of the people provoked Pitt's government into the mistaken assumption that ideas which were revolutionary in their implications must be supported by organisations with revolutionary designs, intent on the seizure of power by force of arms. Events in America, France and Ireland, the violence of food-rioting within Britain, strikes aboard merchant vessels and warships over pay and conditions, the violent undertones of the reformers' rhetoric and wartime scares about French subversion, all compounded the government's fears. And it was in this atmosphere that the government found itself compelled to defend the country against the French and its own privileged position against reformers. Not surprisingly there was much misunderstanding and little willingness to compromise. The notorious Lord Braxfield, who presided over the sedition trials in Edinburgh in 1793 and handed out some draconian punishments, detected 'a spirit of sedition and revolt going abroad which made every subject seriously uneasy'. Intended revolt, declared Prime Minister Pitt in the House of Commons, was cloaked by 'the pretext of a parliamentary reform'. To Pitt the British Convention in Edinburgh was an attempt to usurp the established government, to introduce 'a species of tyranny' based on the 'voice of the people'. 'The very name of British Convention carries sedition along with it', charged the solicitor-general at the trial of its secretary, William Skirving. 'It is assuming a title which none but the members of the established government have a right to assume. And the British Convention, associated for what? for the purpose of obtaining universal suffrage; in other words, for the purpose of subverting the government of Great Britain. . . .' [P35; s11, *303, 302*; P6]

In the government's view the French-style title of the Convention and the assembly's modes of procedure and address were at best disloyal and at worst an invitation to revolution. Its dangerous character was magnified by the government's fear of it as an anti-parliament, a rival body to itself, dedicated to the revolutionary demand of universal suffrage. The opening clause of the 1794 Act suspending habeas corpus proclaimed that 'A traitorous and detestable Conspiracy has been formed for subverting the existing Laws and Constitution, and for introducing the system of Anarchy and Confusion which has so fatally prevailed in France.' 'It was as plain as the sun', said William Windham, M.P., 'that what they meant by reform was wildest anarchy'. [s11, *333, 338*; s13, *68*] 'It is true', conceded the solicitor-general, 'they were formidable, not by their numbers, not by their arms, but they were formidable by being an enemy within our bosoms. This, this alone made them formidable.' [P6]

And so the Crown charged leading conventionists with sedition, not treason, with proclaiming disloyal and revolutionary ideas, not plans of armed revolt.

Thomas Hardy was less fortunate in the charge brought against him, but more fortunate in the outcome of his trial. Lord Chief Justice Eyre told the jury that 'Associations and assemblies of men, for the purpose of obtaining a reform in the interior constitution of the British parliament' were not necessarily unlawful. The danger was that they might 'degenerate and become unlawful in the highest degree . . . . A few well meaning men . . . assemble peacably to deliberate on the means of obtaining redress. The number increases, the discussion grows animated, eager, and violent. A rash measure is proposed, adopted, and acted upon. Who can say when this will stop, and that those men who originally assembled peacably, shall not finally and suddenly, perhaps, involve themselves in the crime of high treason?' [s13, *70*] On such a hypothesis no new political initiative could be taken if its every possible outcome was to be imagined and held against it. This was the perfect rationalisation of conservatism, and it served well the self-interest of its proponents as well as the traditions and institutions which they believed themselves to be defending.

If the reformers were preparing the way for a 'democratic tempest' that would wreak havoc in Britain, it was the duty of the government to protect society against the approaching storm. They neglected no precautions that lay within their power, aided and abetted by those among the governed who were influential enough to ostracise those who appeared to constitute a threat. This practice was clearly at work within the Scottish legal profession. The wife of advocate Archibald Fletcher later recalled that 'for several years . . . such was the tenor of liberal principles in Scotland that no man at the Bar professing them could expect a fair share of practice', while another lawyer claimed that 'it was almost giving up business to be seen doing anything for the Friends of the People'. John Craig Millar, son of the Professor of Law at Glasgow University, a young advocate and member of the Friends of the People, lost employment and left for the United States in 1795, 'banished thither by the strong tide of Tory prejudice . . .'. [P38; P6]

In the same year Henry Erskine was dismissed as Dean of the Faculty of Advocates after he had taken part in a public protest and petitioning in Edinburgh against the Sedition and Treason Bills. [s34, *142*] During 1795-6 government agents in Scotland filed reports on gentlemen who attended Whig dinners. [P35; P9]

Defectors from among the educated and well-to-do were least easy to overlook. Thomas Muir was marked out for exemplary punishment because he had openly distributed Paine's works for the 'lower orders'. At his trial the lord advocate made it plain that Muir's crime was all the greater because he was an educated man who 'could be found among villagers, and manufacturers, poor and ignorant, for the purpose of sowing sedition and discontent'. [P6; s17, vol. 13, *1165–6*] Similarly, Thomas Palmer's offences were aggravated in the eyes of the authorities because he was a 'better class' person joining 'the society of low weavers and mechanics'. [P6; s17, vol. 15, *162–4*] The better-class person was normally to be trusted and normally was trusted. The attorney-general tolerated Part 1 of *Rights of Man* because, 'reprehensible' though it was, it was restricted by its price to the 'judicious' reader. He felt compelled to prosecute when Part 2 'in all shapes, and in all sizes, with an industry incredible . . . was either totally or partially thrust into the hands of all persons in this country; of subjects of every description; when . . . even children's sweetmeats were wrapped up with parts . . .'. [s63, *40*; s7, *87*]

But people were believed to be more dangerous than prints in the short term. After the purging of the leadership of the British Convention the government turned its attention to the London Corresponding Society. On 12 May 1794 Hardy was arrested and in the next few days so too were various members of the Corresponding and Constitutional Societies in London and Sheffield. The arrests were made on the suspicion of a plot to usurp government through a Convention linked to armed revolt, and the government hoped to acquire incriminating documents and witnesses. A parliamentary Committee of Secrecy was soon able to declare that a 'traitorous conspiracy' existed and Pitt got his overwhelming majority for suspending habeas corpus. [s7, *119–20*] The pattern was set for a quarter of a century's government policy towards reform movements, and conspiracy would soon follow repression in a sequence quickly to become a familiar feature of British history.

Although the government failed to secure convictions of the English reformers they were intimidated by the circumstances of the prosecutions, and the open reform movement went into temporary decline as it had done in Scotland following the severer results of the trials there. In 1795 the government went ahead with legislation to forbid all large, public meetings without special permit and to class lecture rooms as disorderly houses, and both English and Scottish reformers rallied to a petitioning movement which combined protests against the Bills with calls for peace with France. The ferocity of the government's behaviour dismayed moderate reformers as well as democrats, and in London the Whig Club and Corresponding Society jointly organised a mass demonstration in Copenhagen Fields; the government's attack upon individual liberty of speech and assembly was unacceptable to many shades of opinion. Christopher Wyvill organised a series of county meetings of protest, and Lord Shelburne, in the House of Lords, attacked the Bills as an over-reaction to the 'Jacobin' scares and warned the government that it was wrong to repress the symptoms of discontent instead of redressing grievances. [s7, *152*; s11, *293-5*]

The meetings and petitions provided a popular outlet for open protest against the Pitt regime, but they hardened rather than softened the government's policy of meeting agitation with coercion. Widespread food-rioting and the mobbing of the king's coach in London in October 1795 added to the government's determination to take strong measures. The Portland Whigs had come over to Pitt in early 1794, and, with the parliamentary opposition gravely split and the extra-parliamentary reform organisations intimidated by arrests and trials, the government ignored the 1795 protests and passed its Sedition Bills into law. The authorities, sometimes with the help of Loyalist associations, harried the radical reformers who remained active, the Corresponding Societies lost their members and their funds, and the peaceful reform movement declined as it was denied open channels of protest. Secret organisations were outlawed by the 1797 Unlawful Oaths Act, and the 1799 Corresponding Societies Act 'utterly suppressed and prohibited' the United Englishmen, United Scotsmen, United Irishmen and the London Corresponding Society 'as being unlawful Combinations and Confederations against the Government of Our Sovereign Lord the King, and, against the Peace and Security of His Majesty's liege subjects'. In 1798 a Newspaper Act established a system of registration which would facilitate the prosecution of printers and publishers believed guilty of sedition, and the stamp tax on newspapers was raised to put them beyond the means of the poor. And in 1799 and 1800 occurred the codification of the Combination Laws. It was altogether a formidable array of repressive legislation.

The government prosecutions and repressive Acts of 1793-1800 coincided with the early years of the protracted war with France and might be justified as the reaction of a wartime administration intent on tightening political control at home to avoid dissent weakening the war effort abroad. If members of Pitt's government were so motivated they were, at the same time, seizing the opportunity to make political capital out of conspiracy scares, not only to intimidate the extra-parliamentary opposition but also to split the opposition within parliament. Fears of reform were probably deliberately exaggerated, and there was probably

an element of pure political calculation in the manœuvres o
ment. At the same time there was a belief that the contro
stirred up by the reformers might well lead to a re-enactme
of the sequence of events so dramatically worked out in _ __
repressive legislation was pre-emptive, based on fears of what might
occur rather than what was actually happening, but it would be rash to
deny that the fears were genuine.

The irony of these policies is that they helped to create the very
problem that they were designed to solve. The reformers' public meetings, their open organisations, and their extra-parliamentary criticism
of the established order were the alternative, the antidote, to secret
conspiracy and revolt. As long as protest remained open and within the
law it was safe. When it was placed outside the law and driven underground it became dangerous. Only when prosecutions and new legislation inhibited and intimidated the open reform agitation did a minority
of diehard reformers go underground to plan the very revolts that the
government had feared and which their policies were intended to eliminate. The pattern emerged in 1794, was clearly established in 1797, and
repeated itself with remarkable consistency during the post-war period.

On the dispersal of the British Convention, several of its former
members turned their hands to armed conspiracy. Their plot was dis-
covered by chance when Edinburgh law officers stumbled on a cache of
pikeheads and battle-axes while searching the home of a bankrupt. The
plot to start a rising in the city had been laid by a former government spy
and wine merchant, Robert Watt, who had been volunteering information on reformers to the Scottish authorities until the middle of 1793.
His associates were David Downie, a goldsmith, together with about five
other survivors of the Convention. They were ostensibly collecting funds
to finance delegates for a renewed Convention that was to meet in
England, but in reality planning a revolution. Watt's proposal to his
small circle of fellow conspirators was summarised thus:

> In the night time a fire was to be lighted at the Excise Office to
> attach the soldiers from the Castle, and when they were to march down
> the street to aid in extinguishing it, then were the Friends of the People
> to attack and massacre them. . . . This done, the Castle was to be
> taken possession of, together with the Banks and all the public offices.
> The judges and magistrates were then to be seized and imprisoned,
> and when all this was accomplished, a proclamation was to be issued,
> ordering all farmers to bring their grain immediately to market, and
> ordering that no country gentleman should go three miles from home,

all under penalty of death. This was to be followed by an address to His Majesty ordering him to dismiss his Ministers and dissolve the Parliament. [P6]

John Fairly, a builder and a former member of the British Convention, told the court that Watt had said that 'he had no fear of the soldiers, for he would just speak to them, and they would be as glad of freedom as we can be'. Fairly travelled with handbills to Glasgow, Paisley, Kirkintilloch and Stirling to win over the surviving branches of the Friends of the People to a rising. He had little success, although he did report that Paisley was 'in a state of readiness' and that 4000 pikes were supposed to be to hand in Perth; money, he noted, might be had from Stirling but 'Cge. not great, Sppt. as yet not certain'. A non-supporter, Dr Forrest of the Stirling Friends of the People, recalled: 'From the conversation I had with Fairley, I gathered there was to be a rising of the people, and seizing of soldiers' arms.' But there is no clear evidence that branches were willing to co-operate and Stirling's caution was probably typical. Watt was executed on 16 October though Downie was reprieved. The prosecution had failed to establish any connection with the English reformers currently awaiting trial. Neither the armed groups that were believed to exist in London nor the Sheffield artisans who had commissioned pikes to protect themselves against loyalist raids could be shown to be implicated in this plot or to be initiating their own. [P6; s10, 7–8, 13–14, 19–20, 24–5; s7, 126]

The next incitement to the planning of armed rebellion was to come from Ireland. The famine year of 1795 gave a new lease of life to the reform societies, but they soon fell back under the weight of persecution and the disadvantage of being denied open means of protest. The initiative passed to small groups of United Englishmen and United Scotsmen, formed in imitation of the republican United Irishmen.

The United Irishmen had been founded in Belfast in 1791 under the leadership of Wolfe Tone, a Protestant, and the society had aimed to enlist Protestants and Catholics alike in an attempt to gain radical reform of the Irish parliament and to combat English influence. Much of its inspiration was nationalist, and its struggle was soon to become one for liberation from the occupying English, factors which separated it from the reform movements in Scotland and England. Thomas Muir had carried an Address from the United Irishmen to the Scottish Convention in Edinburgh in 1792, but members had rejected his republicanism and his nationalism: Scots reformers were not struggling to free an occupied country but were intent on playing their part with English reformers in democratising the political processes that operated through Westminster. Despite Muir's continued efforts before his arrest in 1793 the Irish and Scottish movements were incompatible in aims and methods, and little headway was made.

Only when the reformers throughout Britain had had their open organisations suppressed did the United Irish find a toehold among small underground groups on the mainland, and these were but a tiny remnant of the reform movement. Irish immigrants appear to have carried their ideas over to Scotland. Irish-style oaths were reported as being administered during 1797 in Ayrshire, Perth and Dundee, but although 'there are a considerable number of disaffected at Perth and still more in Dundee . . . at the same time they in general are not disposed to go into the Irish System' which among the disaffected 'is termed *planting Irish potatoes*'. Among the planters was one James Craigdallie, an Irishman settled in Perth, who administered oaths and was given to wild boasts. He was reported to have claimed 'that in the West Country (around Glasgow) and Ayr they were pursuing the true Robertspierrian System, for if any man deserted the Cause there or betrayed it, *he was never more heard of*'. The informant judiciously added, 'What credit is to give to this I leave you to determine'. [P23; P21] Although later accounts mention a national committee in Glasgow and evidence points to some oath-taking in Ayrshire, most United Scotsmen activity was centred on Perth and Dundee and the adjacent counties of Perthshire, Forfarshire and Fife. A Dundee weaver, George Mealmaker, previously active in the Friends of Liberty and the British Convention of 1793, was the main instigator of oath-taking in Tayside. He had drafted the address for which Palmer had been transported in 1793 and had presided over two sessions of the Convention in the same year. Now as secretary of the Dundee Society of United Scotsmen he was arrested towards the close of 1797 in possession of letters from secretaries 'in other places'. In Cupar, Fife, ten men, including a schoolmaster, were arrested on suspicion of administering oaths and plotting to overthrow the government. [P6; P61]

Mealmaker was transported for fourteen years, having been convicted of taking a leading part in the United Scotsmen's secret organisation 'to excite a spirit of disloyalty to the King, and of disaffection to the existing laws and constitution of Great Britain'. He had sent copies of a United Scotsmen constitution to several places and organised a 'delegate' meeting within his area. Two Dunfermline weavers were tried with him, one of whom was transported for five years; the other was outlawed, having fled the jurisdiction of the courts. [P68; P21] No charges of arming were brought against the men who stood trial, but they were found guilty of organising an underground movement which the government feared could lead to revolt, and they did make some effort to enrol members of the armed forces. After the arrests and trials of 1797–8 the United Scotsmen lingered on until 1802 but made no attempt at a rising and were at no time able to claim any popular support, even in the eastern counties where they were most active. And they failed totally to capitalise on the widespread popular riots of 1797 against militia conscription in Scotland.

Just as men such as George Mealmaker had gone underground from the Friends of the People in Scotland, so did a few members of the London Corresponding Society form the United Englishmen. While the main body attempted to keep up a public, open avowal of reform, some of its supporters, including Irishmen John and Benjamin Binns, were now trying to model an underground organisation on the United Irishmen. As the Irish rebellion gathered momentum in 1798 and Thomas Muir, now returned from Botany Bay to Paris, conspired with Irish exiles to try to mount a French invasion, the government went into action. John Binns visited Dublin and on his return was arrested with the United Irish emissaries. One of the delegation, Father Quigley, was found in possession of a letter from the 'Secret Committee of England' inviting Napoleon to invade England. Such Committee as there was, a rump of Corresponding Society members, were arrested in April 1798 and with that the tenuous beginnings of an Anglo-Irish conspiracy collapsed. The Irish fought alone, and French aid came too sparsely and too late. [s57, *186–8*; s38, *128*]

The collapse of the conspiracy did not mean the disappearance of would-be conspirators, for there was always, it has been suggested, from this time onwards some little group at work somewhere who talked and dreamed of revolution but whose aspirations were not necessarily formalised in the shape of an actual plan of revolt. This is the beginning of the so-called period of the secret, underground tradition, which historians have found so difficult to locate and identify with any precision. Informers testified to its existence, and hints, rumours and clues add up to a mystery that has so far kept most of its secrets intact. Few would deny the probability that there were a few aspiring revolutionaries in Lancashire, the West Riding, the English Midlands and Scotland who escaped detection and arrest and continued to meet in secret and talk and hope of political fulfilment, without ever taking practical steps towards its realisation. Perhaps, as the informers suggested, there were as many as thirty organisations in Lancashire in 1797 which had tenuous links with other societies of similar inclination in other parts of the country, and perhaps increasing persecution and being driven beyond the law urged them more and more towards thoughts of revolution. Perhaps, too, the societies of Manchester were the first to recruit the new factory operatives and to give English Jacobinism its own natural setting of an urban, industrial community that would add social content to the preoccupation with political rights that had so far dominated British radicalism. If so, they were a portent for the future, however tentative and elusive their political role in Britain of the 1790s. The quantification of the membership of the secret groups is an impossible task, though there can be little doubt that numbers were very small. [s57, *189, 191*; s67, *107–11*]

An easier undertaking is a comparison between the situation which launched the United Irishmen into activity across the sea and that which immobilised the tiny groups of United Scotsmen and United Englishmen on the mainland. In Ireland there was a mass base for rebellion and that was the peasant revolt, an element totally absent from the Scottish and English situation, and the Irish masses and their leaders were already part of a long tradition of insurrection against the foreign occupier. Theirs was an independence struggle that adopted republicanism as a direct alternative to the monarchy of the occupying power just as the American colonists had done. It was the nationalism and republicanism of the French Revolution, rather than its democratic aspects, that fired the Irish rising. Instead of rationalistic, often atheistic, doctrines of the French Revolution, the Irish rebels had a Roman Catholic creed to oppose to Protestant Britain, and though Protestants such as Wolfe Tone and Henry Joy McCracken remained important rebel leaders the United Irishmen drew their mass support from the Catholic peasantry, especially after Catholic–Protestant clashes in Ulster in 1795 and the formation of the Orange Order.

In England and Scotland there were no such grounds for an independence struggle, no widespread counter-ideology such as Ireland's Catholicism to underpin revolt. Scotland was no conquered country but one united with her fellow Protestant neighbour under a Scottish king, enjoying formal union with England, and the advantages of economic integration. In Britain south of the Highlands there was nothing to match the sharpness of Ireland's religious and socio-economic cleavage between landlords and peasants, and, apart from the Highlands, Britain was moving towards an industrial economy that contrasted with the peasant structure of most of Ireland. This gave her a much more complex social structure made up of a multitude of overlapping interest groups, in contrast to the simple basic division between the separated and antagonistic interests of peasants and their lords. Catholicism, nationalism and peasant grievances stirred in the Irish an intensity of alienation that excited and legitimised mass revolt. There was nothing comparable in mainland Britain to turn reform agitation towards rebellion and revolution. War with France left the reformers to contend with a formidable 'King and Country' sentiment, whereas England's difficulty was, not for the sole occasion in her history, Ireland's opportunity. In consequence of all these factors the Irish overtures to the Scots and English reformers were either spurned or met with acceptance among only the underground remnants of the open reform organisations. The oaths of the United Englishmen and Scotsmen were far more terrifying than their numbers or their arms, and no mass following heeded their call to rebellion.

One member of the United Englishmen, Colonel Despard, arrested in April 1798, was to re-emerge as leader of a new conspiracy in 1802 and suffer execution in February 1803 for high treason. There is evidence of surviving and active secret societies in being in Lancashire and Yorkshire during the years 1800–3, of oath-taking and talk of revolution. The government, again feeling itself under pressure in 1801, reverted to Committees of Secrecy and a further round of repressive legislation, and the so-called 'Black Lamp' was thought to be swearing in men in the West Riding and preparing them for rebellion. Two Sheffield men were given transportation sentences in the autumn of 1802 for administering secret oaths: they had allegedly been members of an extensive organisation that was arming and preparing itself for a rising. In November Despard was convicted in London along with associates and tried for treason. His commitment to the cause of his native Ireland and to political Jacobinism had earlier taken him into the ranks of the United Irishmen and United English. After his release from prison his additional personal grievances over nepotism in military promotions had led him towards attempting the construction of a revolutionary army which would act alongside the rebel organisation which he supposed to exist outside London and in co-operation with Napoleonic landings which would help rally 'myriads' of Britons to a British revolution. There is no means of knowing whether the Despard plot was essentially the work of a passionate but quite unrealistic conspirator or whether it was to some extent the outcome of a more extensive underground network that incorporated the industrial worker as well as the London tavern scene; this must remain a matter for speculation. It would, however, be fair to suggest that Despard and his guardsmen conspirators had little in common with the discontents of the urban working classes and that their conspiracy should more properly be seen as the last of the Jacobin efforts than as the first of those nineteenth-century designs which had their origin in worker grievance and their location in the provinces. But, however categorised, it had no mass following. [s57, *189, 524–5*; s67, *110*; s38, *128*; p20]

It would, indeed, be difficult to argue that there was any popular political consciousness during this period unless it is to be found in the 'sub-political' responses of the 'Church and King' mobs who directed their fury against Dissenters, reformers or the rich, especially if the last happened to embrace the first two categories. This violent conservatism directed against religious and political dissent also contained a strong element of xenophobia, and the outbreak of war against France strengthened popular patriotism as an antidote to reform agitation, which the government and a host of pamphleteers smeared as unpatriotic and a dangerous Fifth Column. [s47, *135–47*] Throughout Britain the advent of war rallied crowds to celebrate such victories as there were. A Paisley weaver recalled that 'as victories occurred, illuminations and thanksgiving days and rejoicings came in regular succession'. In such an atmosphere reformers were readily identified with French ideas and smeared as traitors. [p53] 'Jacobinism was a term denoting everything alarming and hateful', recalled Henry Cockburn, and the extravagances of the crowds were not concerned with the overthrow of the government but with ugly assaults on the supposed enemies of 'Church and King'. [p35] The spontaneity of the loyalist riots remains an open question. Professional, hired thugs were undoubtedly an element in some areas, and in Manchester, Birmingham and Nottingham magistrates gave tacit consent and encouragement to the mobs by their slowness in intervening in riots and allowing the mob to rampage freely against nonconformists of various kinds. It would none the less be wrong to suppose that such crowds were always artificially contrived. The 'Church and King' mobs were a political response from the lower orders, albeit a crude, emotional and unreasoning reaction, and if they were soon to disappear from English life they were reincarnated in the jingoists of the late nineteenth century, the mobs that persecuted shopkeepers with German-sounding names during the Great War, or those working-class men who have rallied behind racialist demagogues at various times during the twentieth century. Meanwhile the readiness of English crowds to select victims from among those who were trying to lead them towards a new view of politics helped to ensure that the revolutionary cause was preached in the 1790s in spite of the contribution of the crowds rather than with their backing.

Yet the crowds could and would be fickle in their political loyalties. Thomas Hardy's house was ransacked while he was awaiting trial, yet his acquittal was received by popular demonstrations in his favour. Henry Dundas saw the main cause of the riots in 'the levelling principle' which was infecting the lower classes, and he regarded the mobs as more of a liability than an asset to those in authority. Never again would they be so easy to rouse on behalf of the loyalist cause, and by the end of the war they would be widely feared for their radicalism. It is not surprising that Henry Dundas had this greater perception than some of his associates in government, for as political manager of Scotland he had already experienced the unpleasantness of being burned in effigy in Dundee and Aberdeen in the 1790s. 'Church and King' disturbances were in fact unknown in Presbyterian Scotland, and rioters were already adopting radical slogans in the early 1790s against the local loyalist oligarchs who controlled the narrow municipal franchises of the Scottish burghs. Lanark's hereditary provost narrowly escaped shots fired into his house, and Edinburgh crowds threatened to attack the Lord Provost's residence there in celebration of the king's birthday and had to be dispersed by firing troops. In Perth there were even more forthright expressions of disloyalty as crowds took to the streets with 'trees of liberty' and cries of 'Liberty, Equality, and No King'. Despite their greater sympathy for the cause of parliamentary reform than their English counterparts, the Scottish men-in-the-street were condemned by the Scottish Friends of the People for their street tumults and failed to give their apparently greater political consciousness any more substantial expression, either through mass membership of the political societies or through popular backing of any uprising. [s34, *121*; s35, *96, 266-7*]

The most extensive popular movements of those years were not concerned with politics, except indirectly, and these were the food-riots of 1795. In the summer of that year that most characteristic form of action associated with the crowds of pre-industrial England had attained frightening proportions as innumerable districts experienced riots, price-fixing actions by bellicose crowds, the seizure of grain to prevent its movement to other areas and to ensure its consumption locally, and attacks upon the supposed villains of the tragedy, the millers and corn-factors. Law and order were threatened with collapse as a second and greater climax was reached in the autumn and militia units mutinied in some places in solidarity with the rioters. [P16; s67, *99-101*] While Britain waged a war abroad, she was employing both military and naval forces domestically to ensure the movement and protection of supplies. Yet this potentially dangerous situation for the government never assumed real political menace, because the food-rioters remained men apart, quite separate from the movement of political protest and never recruited on behalf of any political movement. They had the force and fury of a revolutionary mob, but they employed them in a cause and manner that were traditional and almost legitimate within English life. The food-rioter was a familiar animal, whose aid was neither obtained nor sought by the political reformer.

More heavy with political menace was the unrest associated with the armed forces, the recruitment riots in Scotland, and the naval mutinies in England in 1797. Under the threat of French invasion the government decided to expand the Scottish militia by what amounted to conscription, and the 'lower ranks of the people' vented their protests during August and September in a series of riots and mobbings extending from and the Borders to Perthshire. These were often a spontaneous response to attempts by the authorities to implement the Militia Act, though news from adjacent areas, sometimes carried by roving mobs, helped to spread the riots. Crowds of up to two thousand disrupted county meetings and mobbed the local gentry, clergy and schoolmasters to force them to destroy the call-up lists and sign pledges not to implement the Act. The rioters were a mixture of miners, shoemakers, weavers, servants, labourers, wrights and occasional shopkeepers and innkeepers. Both men and women were involved. In Tranent, East Lothian, a woman who 'beat the drum to assemble the mob' was killed in clashes with troops, in which eight or nine rioters died and several soldiers were badly injured. This was the most violent incident, but there were others of almost equal ferocity involving clashes between rioters and the armed forces. In spite of their political origin the riots had no political aims beyond the thwarting of the operation of the Militia Act, and they had no links with the United Scotsmen. [P68; P61; P23; P21]

Similarly, in England, unrest among the sailors of the war fleet remained apart from the emergence of the United Englishmen, and their grievances concerned wages, food, living conditions and impressment, however tempting it might be to link their emergence with the political campaigns of the time. On 18 April 1797 delegates from Royal Navy vessels at Spithead petitioned parliament for better conditions after the failure of appeals to commanders, the petitioners professing their loyalty to the king and readiness to defend their country. Within a month disputes were settled and the fleet left for war duties. In June delegates from ships at the Nore made similar demands, not unaware of what might be read into their protests: 'Let his Majesty but order us to be paid and the little grievances we have made known redressed, we shall enter with alacrity upon any employment for the defence of our country. . . . We do not wish to adopt the plan of a neighbouring nation [France], however it may have been suggested. . . .' [P68]

This protest acquired more formidable proportions in spite of the assurances of the men. The Nore fleet, joined by Duncan's fleet that had been barring the Dutch fleet's invasion route to Britain, hoisted a red flag, declared a 'Floating Republic', and prepared to blockade London until their demands were met. On the settlement of their grievances the sailors declared their thanks and their loyalty and restored the British flag. Government investigators reported 'with great confidence that no . . . connection or correspondence ever did exist' between mutineers and reform or republican groups or individuals on shore. They were probably right, though they would not have been very ready to admit to political disaffection within the fleet even had it existed. [P68; s13, 73-4; s38, 27-8; s7, 156-7; s31]

And this remained the pattern of popular grievances that were ventilated during these years: they arose from precise and readily identifiable causes, food shortages, militia conscription or conditions of service, and could assume formidable proportions, as did a further round of widespread food-riots in 1800, and pose grave threats to law and order. Yet for all that they remained quite apart from the political movement, which made no attempt to exploit social and economic discontent for political advantage. Henry Cockburn was later to reminisce that 'the lower orders seemed to take no particular concern in anything' as he looked back over the period of the 1790s. [P35, 45] This was an over-statement which ignored both the diversity of 'the lower orders' and the range of issues that had troubled them, but it did hint at the predicament of the parliamentary reformer who was endeavouring to create a mass movement among people whose everyday concerns were not the workings of the political system. The wish of the reformers to pose a long-term challenge to the whole political structure was almost totally remote from the real lives of the actual people who made up the unenfranchised, people who experienced far more discontent and suffering from high food prices than they did from the denial of their political rights. By the turn of the century the cause of political reform had still not reached the people in any great numbers.

It can be seen in retrospect that reform would not become a mass movement until it shifted both its geographical base and its social centre of gravity. Although London would remain a principal centre of political movements in the nineteenth century, it came to be rivalled in importance by the industrial centres of the North and Midlands. In Scotland the shift from Edinburgh and the eastern counties to Glasgow and the western ones is more dramatic and complete. In social terms this meant, in England, that the aristocratic patrons and the artisans would be joined by more obviously proletarian elements; in Scotland the Whig lawyer would cease to be the characteristic figure in reform politics and would be supplanted by the weaver. In other words, the reform movement, which acquired so much of its political inspiration from the French Revolution, would become a popular movement only through the consequences of the Industrial Revolution. And the reason why industrialisation did not create a mass political movement earlier is not simply that it was insufficiently advanced by 1800 but that its early decades generated fair prosperity and created for many who participated in its early progress what was later to appear something of a 'golden age'. The end of the century was to be a turning-point for large groups of industrial workers who were later to be actively associated with political movements, the weavers and framework-knitters for example, and falling wages and declining standards would cause them to explore the various options open to them. Meanwhile the economic basis for popular discontent and mass political interest was lacking, and those who did suffer focused their protests upon the problems of day-to-day existence rather than on the grander designs of political reformers. And so there remained the contrast between, on the one hand, the protesters' diverse and localised reactions to specific grievances and events, and, on the other, the reformers' attempt at a national challenge to the entire political system. And in so far as there was a cause which captured men's hearts it was not that of reform, nor even Methodism, but the war with France that could rally broad cross-sections of the population. And this was a cause for the government to proclaim. Invasion scares and victory celebrations diverted the populace into patriotic dispays that further isolated the reformers as 'disloyal Jacobins'. Before they could be successful the reformers needed to address larger economic and social groups than those who had listened to their message in the eighteenth century; they needed the means of communicating their message, and this the government was fairly effectively denying in the 1790s, and they needed their audience to be suitably receptive. These conditions would soon come much nearer to being fulfilled, though the reformers would continue to face the problem of how to agitate public opinion without hardening government reaction to the point of suppression of open reform organisations.

In the meantime policies of repression drove a few individuals to the desperate recourse of talking about and sometimes even plotting armed revolt, and the few small armed groups that did exist were the product of the breakdown of the open reform agitation rather than part of its strength. But the revolutionary groups never exploited or directed the militia or food-rioters or the threats of the mutineers. Successful exploitation of the latter in particular could have been damaging for the government; it might well have shaken their control at home as well as opening the way for Dutch and French invasion; in combination with an armed reform movement in Britain this situation could have been very serious. In fact an armed 'Fifth Column' never existed within Britain, and the few armed plotters who did exist bequeathed to their nineteenth-century successors the problem of how to emerge from underground isolation into open, co-ordinated, and widespread revolt. If they remained secret no one knew of their activities and a mass following was impossible. If they publicised their activities they were arrested and their plans collapsed. In the eighteenth century they remained too isolated, too weak in numbers, arms, and co-ordination, too inexperienced in actual rebellion, to be able to overcome the problem of converting closed conspiracy into open revolt. It remained to be seen whether this dilemma was capable of being resolved.

2 Luddites, Hampden Clubs and the Pentrich Rebels

In February 1803 a former army officer, Edmund Despard, was hanged in London for high treason. In October 1817 a former stocking-knitter, Jeremiah Brandreth, was hanged in Derby for the same crime. The occupation and lower social status of the second man, and his geographical area of activity, are all worth noting, as well as the fact that he actually led a revolutionary army in the field. They reflect important changes that were taking place in these years within each of the areas previously considered. Popular movements, previously local and unco-ordinated responses to grievances that were themselves often local, were becoming almost national in scope and acquiring organisation. The political movement, previously the preserve of a small minority, often artisan groups in old centres of population, and concerned primarily, almost exclusively, with political rights, was acquiring a mass following and becoming a popular movement, identified increasingly with the new industrial districts and owing its rise and strength to social discontent as much as political grievance. Government policies of repression rather than reconciliation remained a consistent feature of the overall picture, though they became increasingly unacceptable and dangerous because of the greater numbers now dissatisfied and their greater degree of organi-sation. And the revolutionary minority, though still very much a minority, became more active, probably more numerous, and did, at last, stage an actual attempt at revolution where soldiers were required to suppress insurgents who had a declared intent of changing the government by force.

In the late eighteenth century the popular movements, especially the characteristic food-riot, were little more than a local threat to law and order, and unless they arose from discontent within the armed forces were scarcely heavy with political menace. In the early part of the nine-teenth century they took on a new scale, acquired a new scope, and developed various characteristics that made them more ominous in the eyes of those in authority and potentially more able to serve the purpose of revolution within British society. The most important of these were trade unionism, which began to exercise an important role within manufacturing industries, and Luddism, a violent form of industrial protest which erupted in three separate areas and industries in 1811–12 and offered nightmarish suggestions of the kind of threat that a discontented industrial work-force could pose to society.

In spite of the Combination Laws of 1799–1800 industrial organisation did develop amongst the cotton handloom-weavers in an attempt to resist the decline that they were experiencing from the turn of the century. These domestic workers of Lancashire and the West of Scotland found their cottage industry deprived of the last vestiges of protection with the lapsing of the Apprenticeship Acts and their eventual repeal in 1813-14. Their trade was flooded with the surplus labour of every other calling, and because weaving was a relatively unskilled job, easy for anyone to learn, it became the aim of Irish immigrants into Liverpool and Glasgow, refugees from the countryside, the unemployed from every occupational group, and the work-force expanded out of all proportion to the orders available from the 'putters out'. When foreign trade was interrupted the outworkers became trapped in the vicious circle of cut-price work, longer hours for lower prices and the consequent exacerbation of under-employment and unemployment. Unable to stem the rise of their own numbers they petitioned parliament for the enforcement of the Apprenticeship Laws to close off one source of cheap labour and coupled with this a request for a legal minimum wage. The growing amenability of parliament to the doctrines of political economy ensured that their appeals would go unanswered, and after the third Minimum Wage Bill, like its predecessors of 1795 and 1800, was decisively defeated in 1808, a widespread weavers' strike broke out in Lancashire in that year. There were further vain appeals from the weavers for state regulation in 1809 and 1811, and the machine-breaking incidents in Lancashire and Cheshire during the months of January–April 1812 took place against a background of attempts by weavers' committees to persuade employers to abide by wage agreements. [s51, 137, 140, 207; s45, 14; s23, 57–87; s13, 84–5]

In Glasgow a delegation of weavers petitioned the Lord Provost, Kirkman Finlay, in January 1812, 'to affix a reasonable rate of wages in the cotton manufacture', which he refused to do, being himself a leading cotton manufacturer, and in spite of securing the approval of the Scottish Court of Session for their wage proposals they were ignored by the employers. In despair, weavers' delegates from eighty Scottish towns and villages decided in November 1812 'not to work under the rates declared reasonable by law', 'scarcely the sound of a shuttle being heard from Aberdeen to Carlisle' for nine weeks. The authorities abandoned their professed policy of non-intervention; troops were mobilised, strike leaders arrested and the strike collapsed, leaving the problem of falling wages and rising labour influx as acute as ever. [P55; s51, *398*]

Despite their failures these early attempts at trade union pressure were claiming a wider spread in terms of numbers and areas involved, and a degree of organisation was beginning to appear as regional structure, with occasional correspondence or 'delegate' visits between regions, began to develop. During 1809–12, according to a Glasgow weavers' leader,

> the large towns were divided into districts, consisting of a certain number of looms; each village forming a distinct district; these districts were again sub-divided, according to circumstances, and one or more persons appointed to superintend them; the whole of whom formed a local committee, with power to call general meetings, when any exigency required. Central committees – composed of delegates from a number of districts – were formed, in Scotland, Bolton, Preston, Carlisle, etc. and, in Ireland, at Belfast, between whom a constant and active correspondence was kept up. [P55, *13*]

Almost certainly the organisation was far less complete and smoothly operating than this account suggests, but it is indicative of a state of affairs far removed from the crude, uncoördinated protests of food or militia riots in the nineties. In Glasgow, it was said, regular weekly meetings were held, and 'the greatest anxiety was shown to conduct every thing legally, the crown lawyers being furnished with printed copies of the articles and regulations'. [P55; s13, *94–9*]

A similar care and caution was taken by the East Midlands stockingers and lacemakers to try to work within the law and with the approval of the authorities as they too attempted in 1812 to secure parliamentary regulation for trades which experienced, especially in the case of hosiery, many of the problems of the weavers. Working from a Nottingham base, Gravener Henson and his committee mobilised thousands of supporters for a petitioning campaign from various parts of England and Scotland as well as within the immediate counties of Nottinghamshire, Derbyshire and Leicestershire. Henson even visited Dublin to extend the range of his campaign. This enterprising endeavour failed in its central purpose, but it was replaced by an equally remarkable body, the Society for Parliamentary Relief, which set up as a manufacturer in its own right, made some wage gains for groups of its members, financed selective strikes against offending employers, and perhaps even sanctioned some frame-breaking where employers were not otherwise vulnerable. The organisation of this body was said to be modelled on Methodism, with classes throughout the hosiery districts which sent group delegates to the meetings of the central committee. It was essentially the same structure as that of the Glasgow weavers, and it could be argued that, in borrowing from the Methodists, these minor organisations of local groups, led by a regional committee in occasional correspondence with other regions, provided a pattern for the Radical Reformers' post-1815 attempts to convert their mass audience into a mass movement and ultimately into a mass organisation. Nor was it simply a matter of organisational patterns, for the personnel involved in the industrial struggles of these years would themselves form the mass base for political radicalism in the post-war period. [P11; P16]

More alarming to the authorities than experiments in trade unionism and more suggestive of revolutionary intent was the wave of machine-breaking, known as Luddism, which, particularly in 1812, posed so many problems to those responsible for law and order. It was a pheno-menon of the same industries, and the same areas, that were involved in trade union activity; it had very much the same aims and only its methods were different. The campaigns of the weavers and stockingers were paralleled in those years by those of the woollen workers; in 1805–6, for instance, thousands had petitioned against gig mills, machines which threatened the livelihood of the croppers, and for the enforcement of apprenticeship, and strong fears had been expressed at the spread of factories. In 1809 all laws protecting woollen-cloth workers were repealed, and in 1812 the war against cloth-finishing machinery was launched with the justification that "We petition no more that won't do fighting must'. In all three areas of violence, the East Midlands and Lancashire as well as the West Riding of Yorkshire, this was the pattern, that machine-breaking occurred only after a collapse of collective bargaining, petitioning and peaceful negotiation. Whether the same people now began to advocate different methods or whether the frustra-tions of the moderates allowed the militants to seize the initiative is by no means clear. In Lancashire there was evidence given of attempts to form a machine-breaking organisation from within the trades' committees but there is no evidence that such a committee was responsible for any of the attacks that occurred and good reason for supposing that it was not. Insufficient is known of the earlier careers of the Yorkshire Luddite leaders to enable any clear relationship with trade unionism to be established, and the debate on the enigmatic leader of Nottingham trade unionism, Gravener Henson, still rages too fiercely for any reliable verdict on his connection with frame-breaking. [s55, *106–7, 131–8*; s57, *925–34*]

Luddism was industrial in its origins and industrial too in its aims, though many contemporaries supposed that the movement had political intentions and their view has been given some support in recent times. It is unlikely that this was so. In the East Midlands the Luddites engaged in what has been described as 'collective bargaining by riot' and their targets were carefully selected to reflect their very specific grievances: underpayment, the manufacture of allegedly inferior products, the use of unapprenticed labour or truck-payments. In Yorkshire, Luddism was an anti-machine movement and its targets were shearing-frames and gig-mills. In Lancashire its targets were steam-looms, but the relative unimportance of these objects of vengeance at this time suggests that they were almost incidental to what was a more general protest movement arising from distress that derived from low wages, high prices and under-employment. The industrial targets, employers and their property, continued to reflect industrial aims, and there were no assaults on property that had a political significance such as town-halls, courthouses, banks or barracks. Fears that these might occur were never fulfilled, and those who took the most trouble to understand what was happening and to administer the law impartially, George Coldham, town clerk of Nottingham, Conant and Baker, the London police officers who specifically investigated such fears, Fitzwilliam, the Lord-Lieutenant of the West Riding and his most conscientious magistrate, Joseph Ramsden of Huddersfield, all these men became convinced that Luddism originated in economic distress and aimed at economic alleviation and was without political purpose. It remained devoid of any tendencies to develop into a political revolutionary movement, and even on the industrial front it was not demanding a new structure but seeking rather to salvage what it could from the wreckage of the old paternalist, protective legislation. Luddism was more a spasm in the death throes of declining trades than a birth pang of revolution. Its methods and its ideology were both 'pre-industrial' and neither would find a place of importance within the techniques or beliefs of organised workers of the next generation. [s55, *74–100*; s57, *604–59*]

What Luddism did illustrate, and this was in itself alarming enough for the authorities, was a remarkable capacity for organisation within working-class ranks and a remarkable solidarity in the protection of the law-breakers and their secrets. Although Nottinghamshire Luddism began as a collective act of protest by crowds of angry people, it was quickly transformed into a carefully planned operation of smaller, efficiently operating groups which moved decisively against prearranged targets and then disappeared from sight. In terms of sheer administrative efficiency Luddism was a notable demonstration of the possibilities of working-class organisation and protest. In Yorkshire, too, activities were carefully planned and staged, and when the Luddites moved from attacks on small workshops to assaults upon factories, forces of several hundreds were mobilised from different towns and villages to constitute an assault force of no mean proportions. Lancashire Luddism, in this as in so many aspects, was unlike the rest, for machine-breaking here lacked the planning and control of the other areas, and was the work of protest crowds of diverse composition rather than smaller, committed groups organised for the specific purpose. The incidents in Stockport, Westhoughton, Middleton and Manchester, were all vaguely predictable, but their timing and manner of accomplishment were part of no systematic plan. Nor is there any good reason to suppose, in spite of rumour and the reports of spies, that there was any co-ordination between the Luddism of Lancashire, Yorkshire and the East Midlands. The relation of each area's protests to the grievances of specific groups and the industrial context within which they worked meant that the Luddites had nothing to gain from a national link-up as long as their aims were industrial; interregional links would only have been meaningful if some greater purpose had been their aim, and this was not so. Luddite organisation was frightening because of its efficiency and because of its potential; it was not frightening because it actually did link up successful working-class protest groups in different parts of the country who were intent on threatening the government rather than their employers. [s55, *103–38*]

It was also frightening because of the methods that it employed, for Luddism involved the systematic use of organised and controlled violence for the achievement of its aims. It has been shown that violence had an important role to play in working-class bargaining procedures in the age before trade unionism, and violence was a familiar enough feature of crowd behaviour during food-riots and reached almighty proportions during the Gordon Riots of 1780. [s24, *5–17*] But Luddism was something different, for it was widespread, prolonged, but above all controlled in its application, as if violence were a legitimate and usable weapon that could be invoked as and when necessary by the working classes. If this kind of idea should achieve widespread acceptance there might indeed be danger that lessons learned in the field of industrial protest could be applied elsewhere and for more serious purposes.

This was the danger, too, of Luddism as a successful challenge to the law-and-order machinery of the nation. If authority could be flouted with so much success it would lose its credibility and be vulnerable to challenges on other issues. If the routine law-and-order machinery of the country was so strained by Luddism that it needed to be supplemented by 12,000 regular soldiers employed for internal peace-keeping purposes the implication was that the government would not be able to withstand anything more widespread than the threat which the Luddites posed, and their activities were confined to three relatively limited geographical areas. It is not then surprising that the crime wave which accompanied Luddism and probably fed upon its successful example should have been seen as an escalation of Luddism, for which the machine-breakers were to blame, or that the arms raids in the summer of 1812 in Lancashire and Yorkshire should have been seen as the responsibility of the Luddites and a step towards a revolutionary uprising. There is no clear evidence on any of these matters of contemporary and later speculation. Arms thefts occurred only after military violence had been employed against the Luddites and might have been intended for defensive purposes, or to further the general crime wave, or even as a simple gesture of defiance. Some people might have hoped and dreamed of revolution, but there is no evidence that the Luddites were planning revolution, and the rumours of a general rising all went unfulfilled. There is no justification for the claim that, after April 1812, 'the Luddite organisation shifted its emphasis to general revolutionary preparations'. The rumours of a general rising were strongest in Lancashire, the area where no successful Luddite organisation is known for certain to have existed, but where political radicals were most certainly at work promoting schemes of parliamentary reform which inevitably raised the hackles of those who sought to preserve the *status quo*, radicals who earned themselves the name of 'Luddite' according to the current terminology for all makers of mischief. But if magistrates and mill-owners were unable or unwilling to distinguish between social protest and political revolution and unable or unwilling to make discriminating use of the confused and sensational gossip supplied by their informers and *agents provocateurs*, there is less excuse for historians' unwillingness to make this necessary distinction. It is understandable that contemporaries should have frightened themselves with these thoughts, for the apparent breakdown of law and order was frightening, but there is no evidence to suppose that the Luddites hoped to exploit this for anything other than limited, industrial aims. [s55, *141–57*; s57, *604–59*]

It is inconceivable that some former Luddites should not have

espoused other causes when their own collapsed, and some might well
have found themselves caught up in the post-war revolutionary movement in later years. The oft-quoted remark of the Derbyshire magistrate
in 1817 that the Luddites had largely turned to 'politics and poaching'
is in no way surprising. [P14] If they were, as he alleged, 'principal
leaders in the Hampden Club', this indicates no more than that many
former machine-breakers had turned towards the parliamentary reform
movement, and it cannot be assumed that they belonged to the extremist
wing of the movement, prepared to carry over their industrial violence
into politics. George Mellor, the Yorkshire Luddite executed for the
murder of William Horsfall, a mill-owner, could have had little to lose
by advocating revolution as he awaited trial. Instead he wrote from his
York cell in support of a petition, a distinctly non-violent political
means, which he had heard was being prepared in favour of parliamentary reform. [P16] This one case does not, of course, enable the
argument to be raised that the Luddites as a whole had moved towards
political consciousness by the end of their abortive industrial campaigns,
but it does indicate the willingness of one Luddite leader to accept the
initiative of those who were currently seeking to mobilise the working
classes on behalf of the reform movement.

Jacobinism died with Despard but political reform was to re-emerge
in England within a few years of his death. The final defeat of French
invasion schemes in 1805, the death of Pitt in 1806, the creation of the
Ministry of All the Talents, including Foxite Whigs, and the disillusionment that this produced, all these prompted the reappearance of a
reform movement which had its first successes in the popular constituency of Westminster. Here voluntary organisation and canvassing
among the journeymen voters, masterminded by Francis Place in a role
made to measure for him, resulted in the election of two reformers, Sir
Francis Burdett and Lord Cochrane, to the borough's two seats. Westminster was established as a stronghold of parliamentary radicalism for
years to come, and the reformers' success helped to revive interest elsewhere, but the triumph was of limited importance for the reform movement as a whole. The popular nature of the franchise and the strategic
siting of the constituency allowed the peculiar talents of an extraordinary
body of men to come together for the first time, but the success of
Burdett, Place, Cobbett, Cartwright and Hunt in this special area did
not necessarily foreshadow similar triumphs elsewhere. [s13, *78–81*;
s57, *502–7*] Their methods here offered no prescription for bringing the
masses of the unenfranchised North and Midlands into a movement
that might create more popular constituencies. That was to be provided

by economic discontent. It was already turning desperate social protest into an organised, almost a national, force. It was about to turn the political reform movement for the first time into a popular movement, as thousands of workers, especially in declining branches of the textile trades, turned to the cause of radical reform for salvation. The coming together of reform and popular protest sets the early nineteenth century apart from the period of the nineties, when the two followed separate, independent courses.

A Paisley weaver recalled the impact of the accumulated failures of pleas to the government, industrial action and the coming of peace:

> All the operatives here expected that peace would have the effect of raising wages. Quite the reverse, however, was the consequence; wages fell rapidly, and in the course of two months the price of weaving was reduced by one half, and the number of soldiers who were returning home aggravated the evil. Peace before this was expected to be the grand panacea to cure all evils, now the great cure was to be radical reform. [P53]

The cynicism came only after further disappointment. As early as 1812 Major Cartwright had visited Nottingham and asked for permission to hold a public meeting to try to persuade the framework-knitters to abandon frame-breaking and work for parliamentary reform as the solution to their economic problems, thereby implying a link between political and economic conditions that the political economists were increasingly determined to deny. [P67] The assumed link was nevertheless important to those working men who rallied to the cause, and Samuel Bamford, the Middleton weaver, was to recall how the reform campaign emerged as a mass movement amid widespread popular unrest and disillusionment at the collapse of peace into post-war depression: 'whilst the laurels were yet cool on the brows of our victorious soldiers on their second occupation of Paris, the elements of convulsion were at work amongst the masses of our labouring population. . . .' Demonstrations and riots greeted the introduction of the Corn Laws. Bridport and Bideford rioters cried out against the high price of bread and the exporting of grain, while in Dundee the high price of meal provoked tumults and the plundering of shops. Unemployed farm labourers in East Anglia expressed their plight by attacking agricultural machinery, while Luddism erupted for the last time in the East Midlands. Economic distress was also at the root of a soup-kitchen fracas in Glasgow and of disturbances in Preston, Walsall, Merthyr Tydfil and Newcastle upon Tyne. Amid this diverse and scattered unrest, recorded Bamford, the writings of William Cobbett and the petition campaign of the Hampden Clubs proclaimed an all-embracing message, that 'the true cause of sufferings [was] misgovernment' and 'its proper correction' 'parliamentary reform'. [P28; P22] In other words the parliamentary reformers were attempting to comprehend under one banner all the diverse forms of social protest that existed throughout the country and create just one popular movement, that for the reform of parliament. It was an impossibly optimistic aim, perhaps coming nearest to fulfilment with Chartism, but it did establish parliamentary reform as one of the great working-class aims over many years, and it did give the reform movement the mass base which it had previously lacked.

The instrument of this transformation was the Hampden Club, founded in London in 1812 under the leadership of middle-class and gentlemen reformers such as Cartwright and Burdett. Much of the middle-class following disappeared with the repeal of the income tax in 1816, and the riots and disorders also frightened many away from reform demands, which were beginning to attract lower-class support. Undeterred, the Hampden Club's secretary, Thomas Cleary, and the venerable pioneer, Major Cartwright, embarked on a series of nationwide missionary tours in an effort to channel economic discontent into mass petitions for radical reform. During 1815–16 Hampden Clubs were formed in the Midlands, Lancashire and Yorkshire, and similar clubs were established in Scotland. Cartwright's thirteen-week tour of Scotland in 1815 illustrates the popular acclaim which the reform campaign was now winning in the provinces. The veteran reformer received an enthusiastic welcome as he addressed large crowds in Edinburgh, Glasgow, Dundee, Stirling, Alloa and other centres. By November he had collected 600 Scottish petitions, and numerous local reform societies and committees were being formed in his wake. The estimated 100,000 Scottish signatories contributed to a British total of over half a million during 1816–17. But parliament, impressed still by property rather than numbers, rejected the demands for annual parliaments, manhood suffrage and the secret ballot. [P30; s44, 21, 24; s35, 221]

Failure in parliament was offset by success in the country. Radical reform had won a mass audience, clubs and societies were multiplying and some workers were becoming more 'deliberate and systematic in their proceedings'. The next step was to link up the activities of the groups at regional level and turn into a national movement the large numbers now becoming involved. [P28] Penny subscriptions were gathered by Hampden Clubs in Lancashire and Yorkshire; in Lancashire delegate conferences were convened and Manchester reformers organised a supply of speakers for local clubs, to promote political discussion among their working-class members. In Glasgow reform societies moved from petition-signing to the organisation of a mass open-air meeting at Thrushgrove on the edge of the city on 29 October 1816, when about 40,000 people heard demands for annual parliaments and universal suffrage. There were comparable rallies in Spa Fields, London, during the same period. In this way thousands of the 'lower orders' were given a means of participating in the reform movement which had not been available in the conventions of the 1790s. Moreover, the mass meetings peaceably harnessed popular discontent that in the past had dissipated itself to no constructive purpose through local riots and were evidence of the reformers' growing ability to organise disciplined, peaceable mass support. [s28, *48–56, 64*; s19, *102*; s13, *130*]

In the autumn of 1816 Major Cartwright called for renewed and widespread petitioning to focus the power of the new mass audience upon parliament, and the campaign culminated in the celebrated gathering of delegates from London and the provinces, in particular the north of England, at the Crown and Anchor Tavern in January 1817. Unhappily for their cause personal rivalries marred the proceedings. This was partly a reflection of differences between the advocates of household and manhood suffrage, and partly the problem of achieving harmony between such vain leaders as Cobbett and Hunt. Eventually the democrats triumphed, and Hunt had the honour of bearing the petition to parliament through the excited crowds who had given the Prince Regent a boisterous reception earlier in the same day. Hunt 'unrolled the petition, which was many yards in length, and it was carried on the heads of the crowd, perfectly unharmed'. Outside parliament, according to Samuel Bamford, Lord Cochrane 'took charge of our petitions . . . we . . . bore him on our shoulders across Palace Yard, to the door of Westminster Hall; the old rafters of which rang with the shouts of the vast multitude outside'. [p28]

This marked the climax of this stage in the history of the political reform movement. It was a climax but not a triumph, for the government chose to reject the petitions, unimpressed by the fact that they were the result of widespread peaceful campaigning. The reform movement had again reached a point where it was about to be cut down by a government which, deliberately or through confusion, adopted a mistaken interpretation of the movement, as its predecessors had done in the nineties, and which, again like its predecessors, found itself confronted by a revolutionary conspiracy in place of the open reform movement which it had so determinedly suppressed.

The reaction of the government to the post-1815 reform societies was in some ways more extreme than its reaction to Luddism a few years earlier. True the government had made frame-breaking a capital offence in 1812, approved schemes for the introduction of watch and ward, and deployed huge numbers of soldiers against the machine-breakers; but it had never panicked. Despite the actual violence that the Luddites had introduced into English life, and despite the alarmist reports of panic-stricken magistrates who grimly foretold a general rising, Lord Sidmouth, who replaced Richard Ryder as Home Secretary at the height of the troubles, showed a fair capacity to discriminate between the accurate and the spurious in the reports that reached him. He was well served by the perceptive and cool-headed General Maitland, commander-in-chief of the armed forces in action in the North and Midlands. Habeas corpus was never suspended during the crisis and the government weathered a storm that was real without committing any great folly. But when the reform clubs of the post-war period began to develop correspondence links with each other and interregional 'delegate' exchanges, the government feared that the movement was developing a national organisation and invoked the Seditious Societies Act to intimidate and disrupt the reformers' loose network. The emerging radical press, a potential instrument for integrating the regional groups into a national movement, was similarly harried by local and central government. The old fears returned, if they had ever left, both of the ideology which the reformers were preaching, and the organisation which they seemed capable of building up, a state within a state, a possible machine for the waging of armed rebellion. For their part the reformers were determined to maintain order at their rallies, for to sanction disorder or to be seen to encourage revolt would put at risk their whole emergent structure of clubs, conferences, and mass meetings. In the event the very order of the rallies had the ironic effect of arousing the government's repressive reflexes. A capacity to organise and control was more alarming than the rampages of undisciplined rioters. The democratic message and developing organisation that propagated it were both anathema to the government, which appeared determined to unearth evidence to confirm its fears that reform meant revolution, which it found in armed conspiracies. These could be used to declare the reformers guilty by association and to provide a justification for repressive measures against all extra-parliamentary Radical agitation. With the aid of *agents provocateurs*, it found such examples in both London and Glasgow, though in neither case could organisational links be found between the conspirators and the mass political movement or the rest of the country beyond their respective cities.

The use of spies, who had made a deal of mischief in Lancashire in 1812, was to add considerably to the confusion of the post-war years as men employed in the role of detectives often extended their part to one of provocation, either through their own initiative or with the encouragement of their employers. In consequence they became themselves an additional cause of troubles they were supposedly employed to eliminate. John Castle assisted the government in elucidating the Spencean plot in London to turn the Spa Fields rally of 2 December 1816 into an attack upon the Tower, and he was still available to lend a hand during the Cato Street Conspiracy of 1820. In the west of Scotland the Sheriff of Lanarkshire employed an agent called George Biggar, and former Lord Provost Finlay enrolled a former weavers' strike leader, Alexander Richmond, as his informer, while the military authorities had their own espionage devices. The multiplicity of informers, each working independently of the others, added much confusion, as the Lord Advocate and the Home Secretary were left with the task of drawing conclusions from contradictory reports. [P22; P55] The spies also provided a very convenient whipping-boy for the respectable reformers, such as Lord Grey, who was ready to blame them for every unpalatable rumour associated with the reform movement, such as the report that oath-taking was a practice in some areas. [P63] It does seem certain that Richmond indulged in free-lance provocation, as well as informing, and there was a sworn affidavit in July 1817 from an acquitted prisoner, John McLauchlin, that Richmond had tried to persuade him to organise a committee to plan rebellion. [P69] It was a recurrent theme of Opposition Whig criticism of the government during these years that spies, and, by association, the government and local magistrates, were the instigators of conspiracies. The spies certainly demonstrated the vulnerability of any group to penetration of their ranks and gave the government the excuse it sought to move against mass meetings and the open attempts at national co-ordination of the radical reform movement.

When the Hampden Club presented their mammoth petition in January 1817 ministers ignored the peaceful campaigning that had produced it and professed to see the mobbing of the Prince Regent, the Spa Fields riots, the Glasgow secret societies and the whole reform movement as parts of a general revolutionary danger, Intent on silencing rather than answering the reformers, the government set up a Committee of Secrecy, which reported that 'a traitorous conspiracy has been formed in the metropolis for the purpose of overthrowing, by means of a general insurrection, the established government, laws, and constitution of this kingdom ... and that such designs extended widely in some of the most populous and manufacturing districts'. [P63] Acting on the basis of such ill-founded premonitions, and with no evidence of plans for a general insurrection, parliament quickly suspended habeas corpus. All reform societies and clubs were declared illegal, and the Hampden Clubs and their Scottish counterparts fell into decay. William Cobbett, on the eve of a strategic withdrawal to America, advised his readers 'to have nothing to do with any *Political Clubs*, any secret *Cabals*, any *Correspondencies*; but to trust to *individual exertion* and *open meetings*'. [P30; P59]

A more spirited response came from Manchester, believed to have almost forty Hampden Clubs with some 8000 members within its orbit, whose delegates had talked in London with the Prestons and the Watsons, men involved in the Spa Fields riots. The idea was advanced that thousands of men should begin a march from Manchester to London to carry with them a demand for reform. Upwards of 4000 men gathered on St Peter's Fields, many equipped with bundled blankets for the long trek south, and they have usually been seen as heroic peaceful petitioners, prepared to endure hardship for their cause, though in fact largely dispersed by troops and special constables without ever starting on their way. Neighbouring authorities completed the work of Manchester, for Lord Sidmouth had warned the county magistrates to stop the Blanketeers, and the Duke of Newcastle was later to report with satisfaction that the sole survivor to reach Nottingham had been immediately arrested. The arrests seem an over-reaction to a peaceful demonstration, but the government was not unnaturally apprehensive of the idea of a march from the industrial north, which could possibly gather momentum *en route* to London, where it might arrive as an invading army rather than a group of harmless petitioners. The Prince Regent might receive from such a body something much less acceptable than a mere petition. [P28; P13]

The arrests of large numbers of Blanketeers clearly signalled the government's determination to suppress open reform campaigning. Denied outlets for their grievances, some workers turned to secret meetings, while hundreds more 'slunk home to their looms, nor dared to come out, save like owls at nightfall, when they would perhaps steal through bye-paths . . . to hear the news at the next cottage'. Around Manchester secret meetings were held under the thin disguise of 'benefit societies', 'botanical' groups, and 'relief of the families of imprisoned reformers'. Far from forestalling revolutionary talk, repression had once again had the reverse effect, driving some men to talk of arson attacks, of 'making a Moscow of Manchester', and leaving Samuel

Bamford with a precarious path to tread among conspirators who sought to beguile him. [P28] Not for the first, or last, time the government confused reform with revolution, attempted to avoid the latter by stamping out the former, and in fact brought revolution upon itself by a refusal to tolerate reform movements working within the law. Revolutionary conspiracy throughout the spring of 1817 reached a climax in the Pentrich Rebellion of 9 June, which, because it was one of the very few actual attempts at armed insurrection in nineteenth-century Britain, inevitably commands attention as a main case study of the problems involved in mounting a revolution within this newly industrialising society.

However negligible the strength and organisation of the revolutionaries in Britain at the beginning of March 1817, they were much enhanced by the government's decision to suspend habeas corpus, pick off the known political activists, cause the break-up of the Hampden Clubs and drive the reformers beyond the pale of the law, where they would begin to be the kind of danger to the system that the government professed itself anxious to avoid. According to William Stevens, the Nottingham needlemaker whose leading role in the conspiracy later caused him to flee to America, there had been no thought of resistance until the suspension of habeas corpus; after that no man was safe and desperate situations prompted attempts at desperate remedies. [P59] Oliver the Spy was also alleged to have argued along similar lines at his meetings with reformers throughout the country, that the right of organisation and peaceful petitioning had gone with the loss of habeas corpus, and men were left now with the only alternative of armed resistance. And ironically it was the rump of the Hampden Clubs in Nottingham and Derbyshire, where members had previously been instructed to be 'perfectly legal and constitutional' in their behaviour and to do nothing to disgrace the society, which now provided the administrative structure for plotting an armed insurrection. [P14] A few of them continued to meet, at the public houses of the Derbyshire villages and in Nottingham, thinking perhaps that their ultimate programme of the suffrage and short parliaments remained the same, but prepared now for the use of force as a means of achieving this programme.

Against a background of government repression revolution was planned, not by noisy hordes of demagogues who mobilised the masses, but by a few secretive conspirators. They circulated no seditious publications in Nottingham, according to Major-General Lyon on 13 May; in Derby it was hardly possible to believe in their existence; the meetings of the disloyal in that town, he reported, must be taking place with the greatest possible secrecy since it had not been practicable to discover them. At the same time Major-General Byng was reporting from the West Riding that his part of the country was in a more tranquil state than it had enjoyed for some years. As late as 29 May he was still without the least information of any intention to rise in his area and asked the Home Secretary if his informants were blind or if there really was such intention. [P16] The truth was somewhere between the two; there was no widespread plan to rise, but his informants had failed to detect such conspiracy as did exist. Oliver's letters of early May, with the pardonable exaggeration of a careerist with his way to make, had reported 'much mischief to be apprehended' and 'disaffection spreading daily', which would seem like the normal ploy of the spy were it not for the balanced assessments that he sent in later and the need to counteract the evident complacency of army intelligence in the district. [P14] The conspiracy was real, and it was brought into existence partly through the mistaken notions of the government that repressive policies were a better guarantee of public order than the liberal approach of allowing free expression to political discontent.

It is difficult to establish the precise origins of the particular plan which eventually produced the abortive rising of 9 June. When the House of Lords Committee of Secrecy reported on 19 February on the Nottinghamshire Hampden Clubs that had an avowed object and expectation of nothing less than a revolution, there was no plan in existence to accomplish such a purpose at that time. Yet such plans were being encountered by Samuel Bamford in Lancashire in March, and it was Joseph Mitchell of Liverpool, a well-known figure on Home Office lists, who, according to William Stevens, the Nottingham needlemaker, first broached the scheme as he passed through Nottingham to London in the early part of April. [P28; P59] In London Mitchell was introduced to W. J. Richards, Oliver the Spy, who had successfully offered his services to Lord Sidmouth on 28 March and who had now acquired the contact he needed for introductions to the advanced radicals in the provinces. With the beginning of Oliver's first tour, in the company of Mitchell, who was subsequently arrested in Huddersfield on 5 May, preparations for rebellion began to go forward, though whether Oliver was himself the principal instigator of these plans or whether he was merely reporting on the intentions of others remains a much disputed point. At Wakefield on 5 May Oliver attended a delegate conference of working men from northern and Midland towns, where he learnt of a 'weak and impractical scheme' to launch a general rising later in the month. This was Oliver's own report of the conference. According to all other reports Oliver had himself proposed to this meeting a scheme of insurrection and required all other representatives to declare how many men could be relied upon to rise in the various centres at the appointed hour. For his part he allegedly promised that London would raise 70,000 men in a few hours to support the distressed of the provinces, who must now abandon the policy of petitioning and prepare for war against the borough faction. Whatever its authorship, the plan was to involve simultaneous uprisings in the towns of the North and Midlands, and a concentration of forces around Nottingham prior to a march upon London, where popular support and the solidarity of the soldiers with the cause would ensure that a change of government could be speedily accomplished. [P59; P16; P14]

Among the so-called delegates at Wakefield was Thomas Bacon of Pentrich, a veteran Jacobin of former days, who had attended the celebrated conference of Hampden Clubs in London in January 1817. Bacon, it seems, reported to a committee which sat at Nottingham and remained the principal means, by his journeying to Manchester, Sheffield and other places, of keeping the east Midlands' conspirators in touch with the other expected centres of revolt. [P59] His other function was to organise meetings in a barn at Pentrich, where his own and neighbouring villages could be apprised of the impending revolution and instructed in the need to raise a local army, appoint leaders and procure arms. The choice of Pentrich as the rural focus of the east Midlands uprising was supposedly determined by the close proximity of Butterley ironworks, which the rebels readily assumed could be quickly converted to the manufacture of cannons and pikes. [P2] It seems equally probable that it owed its future fame and notoriety to the accident of being the home of Thomas Bacon, the most active of the conspirators, who would most naturally operate in the area he knew best.

But while the zealots of Pentrich and South Wingfield were contemplating the contribution that Butterley might make to the cause, it was Nottingham that was receiving the visits of Oliver in May and June, learning through its contacts with Sheffield and delegate Crabtree of Bradford that the rebellion was to be postponed until 9 June, and undertaking such practical steps as were taken towards preparing the area for its part in the rebellion. Unfortunately for the prospects of its success, the steps included invitations to one of the town clerk's spies to join the conspiracy and assume responsibility for visiting Arnold, Bulwell, Hucknall, Kimberley and Basford to secure the appointment of reliable delegates in each place and instruct them in the role they were to play. One informer, Abraham Smith, was consulted over plans to attack the local barracks, and invited to state the size of the contingent he was capable of commanding, but he declined such a duty on the grounds that his status as militia private had given him insufficient experience. Another told of their plans to take over the public houses and the arms of the soldiers stationed there, how the district delegates were to retire to their own areas to lead the rebellion there, he to Bulwell, after which they would converge on Nottingham. Oliver found them in the thick of their meetings when he visited Nottingham on 26 May, and his external assessment of their schemes supported the conviction that the authorities must have arrived at by now, that any conspirators who recruited informers so indiscriminately to their cause held out no great threat to their safety. He reported more talk of a determination to proceed with rebellion but the complete absence of any systematic plan for mounting it. There were vague beliefs among the villages that Nottingham would provide the necessary local leadership, while the Nottingham conspirators looked to the supposed stores of arms at Wollaton and elsewhere to see them through their critical period, after which national leaders of the reform movement, such as Burdett or Cobbett, would take command once the first blow had been struck. Belief that local efforts were only part of a nationwide conspiracy was sustained by the encouragement of Oliver, who seemed to confirm that the strength of the movement was at its greatest in those places where he happened not to be at the time of speaking, and by the travelling delegates, such as Bacon and Crabtree, who had less excuse for deluding their fellows and who became intoxicated by the thoughts of the power which they imagined was at their command. [P16; P14]

The emergence of Jeremiah Brandreth as leader of the Pentrich Rebellion is as obscure as many other aspects of the story. He featured in spy reports during May, though not as a potential leader. Bacon introduced Brandreth in Pentrich on the 5th as the man who would lead the local insurgents to Nottingham and at a further meeting at Pentrich on the 6th is reported to have said that Brandreth was a late substitute for a man called Wain, who was to have led them but who was seriously ill. [P16] But whatever Brandreth's status as first- or second-choice leader he was obviously very active and very successful in galvanising the area into activity, visiting Swanwick, acquainting himself with the district, drawing up his plans, and, above all, getting his army to move on the night of the 9th. If explanation is sought as to why the uprising occurred at Pentrich it must be sought in part in the personal achievement of Jeremiah Brandreth. It must also, of course, be sought in the weaknesses of the overall scheme, which had been so successfully penetrated by spies such as Oliver from London, Bradley in Sheffield and Enfield's men in Nottingham, that the authorities had been able to pick off many of the leaders by arresting them and were left to face only a mild rising in Huddersfield on 8 June and the slightly more formidable Pentrich rebellion a day later. Even Nottingham contributed nothing to the rising of 9 June, after Oliver's role had been largely exposed during his hazardous final mission of 7 June, and Pentrich and its neighbours were left to go it alone.

In the light of the failure of the Pentrich Rebellion, it is difficult to attempt anything like a detached assessment of the strategy on which it was based. It was empirically a failure, but there has never been a successful revolution in modern Britain and so it is not possible to examine a successful model. Some nineteenth-century conspiracies, such as Cato Street, envisaged the striking of a decisive blow in London, the seat of government, and establishing revolution in the provinces once the central coup had been delivered. Another approach, the Pentrich approach, was to have provincial movements converging on London and taking over the government once the revolutionary movement had established itself in the country as a whole. It is not possible to say that one approach was better than the other. Both were tried and neither came near to success.

The general strategy of which Pentrich was to be part was fairly clear, though its detail contained many contradictions. Most accounts of what was to have happened allocated Nottingham a central role. The marchers expected to find the town secured for them before their arrival as the officers did not dare to allow their soldiers out of the barracks. They would be met there by 100,000 men from Loughborough, Leicester and other places, and there they would establish headquarters and a seat of provisional government. They would, in some accounts, leave Nottingham for London at the end of the week; in others they were to go down the Trent by boat, take Newark, and then go on to London. [P16; P44] A spy reported on 23 May that the men from Leicester were to retreat to Nottingham, there await those from Yorkshire, and then set out to London, and that men from Lancashire and other parts of Derbyshire would join them on the road. [P16] Yet according to another account at Brandreth's trial the leader had encouraged the countryfolk to join by promising that they would not need to go beyond Nottingham, as London would have fallen by the time they themselves had reached their local capital. [P44] This is not altogether inconsistent with the ideas that Thomas Bacon claimed to have imbibed from Oliver, that simultaneous action throughout the country and the securing of the military (who were alternately described as being so friendly that they did not require to be secured) would enable a change of government to be accomplished without the spilling of blood. Bacon even went so far as to claim that he had 'advanced no violent measures but strictly adhered to what Oliver had laid down at Wakefield'; only at the Assizes had he learned that there had been violence, which had been no part of the original intention. [p14] But Bacon's considerable experience in these affairs suggests that this was a disingenuous rather than naïve account. Most leaders would prefer to win bloodless battles if this were possible, but it would be unrealistic to suppose that a wish to take over arms depots and iron foundries did not indicate a willingness to use force if resistance were made. And it is difficult to believe that there was much expectation that a show of strength would of itself be sufficient to topple the government.

An old-fashioned march upon London seems to have been the clearest and most realistic notion that was commonly held among the rebels, and there was little enough thought given to how that might be accomplished. According to the Bulwell spy, on 23 May Brandreth had suggested that he expected a strike to help him accomplish his purpose, but this is the only reference to this kind of tactic. [p16] Unlike the Scottish conspirators of 1820 the English rebels of 1817 made no attempt to preface their political assault with industrial action, and the great strikes within the local hosiery trade in 1817 and 1819 were quite devoid of political content. This was hardly the movement of a class-conscious industrial proletariat.

If the strategy of rebellion was somewhat obscure the aims of the rebels were even more so. Brandreth's appeal to his followers in the field was designed to make the exercise of waging a revolution as painless and as pleasurable as possible. At Nottingham they would receive plenty of rum and a hundred guineas each, and there would be bread and beef for every man. A band of music would meet them, they would go down the river, and the whole enterprise would be 'like a journey of pleasure'. And afterwards there would be a provisional government formed and sent down into the country to relieve the families of those who had gone away, attending to provisioning, as its function was supposed to be. Captured prisoners on the morning of 10 June repeated these inducements to rebellion that they had heard and vague slogans of 'going a Revolutioning', 'to change the Government and make the times better'; their object was not to plunder but to stand up for their rights and change the government; they would seize all public property, extinguish the National Debt, coin new money, issue new bills and abolish taxes. The whole range of attractions was there for the taking, and every grievance felt by all men about all governments was there for removal.

Some had heard of specific political objectives to be achieved; John Page of South Wingfield, for instance, had heard a fortnight earlier that they must go to London to release some great men who were imprisoned in the Tower of London, another medieval throwback in a modern rebellion; another had heard that a fresh government had been established at Nottingham which they were required to defend. John Bacon, the brother of Thomas, told them *en route* that the government had plundered them of all they ever had and that they must fight or starve, and this theme of hunger was taken up by Thomas Denman in defence, that their object had been to plunder their neighbours' larders and fill their bellies. [P2; P44] Unfortunately for his case the marchers had plundered guns and coerced men, not stolen food, which made his interpretation the less plausible. Nor was it helped by his fellow counsellor, who suggested that the reform of parliament was doubtless what they had in mind. [P44] The slogans of the reformers, manhood suffrage and annual parliaments, had played no part in rousing the rebels, who had certainly suggested fiercer intent by their armed march through the countryside.

Thomas Bacon might have regarded political rights as the ultimate purpose, as he later claimed, but his methods were those of revolution, not reform, and it was the resort to force that gave some sort of coherence and common pattern to the multitude of aims and grievances among the participants. The solicitor's brief for the defence suggested, with good sense, that the plan of revolt as outlined at Wakefield on 5 May and explained to the participants at subsequent meetings was but little understood by most of them, that ignorance and inattention to essentials had drawn them into an affair with no one defined object, only a variety of notions that the law had to be changed and that it might even be possible to achieve this by the act of showing themselves in sufficient numbers. They were to have a revolution which would be all things to all men. [P2]

And the pathos of their hopes and ambitions is increased by the knowledge that their plans were known to the authorities, local and central, who knew fairly accurately the proportions of the danger that confronted them and who had coolly calculated that the rebellion might safely be allowed to proceed without serious threat to public safety to ensure a goodly collection of rebels to put on trial for treason. Oliver's role as chief intelligence agent between one rebel camp and another had ensured that as a national movement the plot must misfire, even had it possessed some inherent strength of its own. Oliver was able to place his stamp of approval upon the local intelligence system on 27 May, when he assured Sidmouth that the local magistrates were in possession of a great deal of information from their agents and knew what was going on. [P14] For once the town and county magistrates of Nottinghamshire seem to have co-operated with each other and shared their information; all the necessary precautions had been taken by 26 May and local arms depots were well guarded, they reported. [P16] When Oliver supplied the last few details on 7 June the magistrates and soldiers had simply to sit and wait, knowing that a harmless enemy was about to deliver itself into their hands.

On the Sunday morning of 8 June Jeremiah Brandreth, by now an open conspirator, held court at the White Horse, Pentrich, seated at a table on which lay a map. [P44; S36] He pointed out to the company, who seem to have come and gone in random fashion through the day, the points where they were to assemble the following night and the route that they would take to Nottingham. The Sheffield and Chesterfield crowds would, he said, join up with them at Butterley. Like Old King Cole, he called for a barrel of gunpowder for the making of bullets and reassuringly, if impractically, promised them that there would be plenty of churches along the route to supply them with lead. The company contained at least two known special constables newly sworn in as a precaution against the expected troubles, one of whom testified against the rebels at their trial. The plans as outlined by Brandreth scarcely smacked of high politics; he and Weightman would go from Pentrich to South Wingfield to meet the Wingfield contingent at Hunt's barn, and they would then meet up with Pentrich people towards Topham's Close. And so it was that Isaac Ludlam the Younger, as he later testified, went to a meeting at about eleven o'clock at night on the 9th and found about forty people there. [P4]

But the meetings were now over and the little bands collected and moved forward, not in some glorious and overwhelming battle array but hesitatingly, with arguments and protests from men reluctantly coerced into the ranks, and with humiliation for Brandreth from the manager of Butterley ironworks, who delivered them a lecture, turned aside the invaders by his words alone, and even dispossessed them of a sack of bullets before seeing them off his premises. Farmers were compelled to give up their guns and households were compelled to contribute to the manpower of the army of revolt, but the pressed men could not be trusted with guns, and the frustrations and disappointments of the march caused Brandreth to lose his temper and fire off his gun through a window, as a result of which a man was killed. With his stature diminished by the unnecessary and cowardly, if accidental, shooting of a man and by his failure at Butterley, Brandreth dispatched Weightman to Nottingham on horseback to report on progress there. His glum countenance on return and Brandreth's refusal to let the man speak for himself reduced the credibility of the announcement that Nottingham had fallen. The coming of rain added damp bodies to already dampened spirits, and Brandreth could keep his army intact only by dire threats against those who tried to flee. In spite of these the force dwindled, and when Lancelot Rolleston, a Nottinghamshire magistrate, appeared at breakfast time on Giltbrook Hill, near Eastwood, at the head of a party of hussars, the rebels fled ignominiously, scattering weapons in all directions as they hurried to hide. Later that day it was reported to the Lord-Lieutenant, the Duke of Newcastle, how Mr Mundy and Mr Rolleston had led out a party of the 15th Regiment of Hussars, consisting of a captain, a subaltern, and eighteen N.C.O.s and privates from the barracks at Nottingham, and Rolleston himself added a hasty postscript that 'a most successful chase' had yielded twenty-eight prisoners, seventeen stand of small arms, and about forty-five pikes. [P13] The Pentrich Rebellion was over and the mopping-up operations could now go ahead.

The massive efforts expended in the tracking down and conviction of those responsible for the rebellion seem to have borne little relationship to the small size of the threat that it posed. Though the authorities in Nottinghamshire and Derbyshire had great difficulty, like some historians, in distinguishing between Luddites and revolutionaries, difficulty which perhaps caused them to exaggerate the menace of the political movements of the immediate post-war years, they knew they had no cause to panic over the conspiracy of May and June 1817. The later claim by William Stevens, that a great part of the population of Nottingham had come to recognise a choice between resistance and slavery during the spring of 1817, is difficult to support in view of the small numbers involved in the Nottingham meetings, the hopeless nature of the organisation they managed to set up, and the almost total apathy of the town during the rebellion itself. The known facts are quite at variance with this extravagant assertion. The townspeople, thought by Rolleston before the event to be more ill disposed than the countryfolk, were not in any way systematically recruited to the cause of revolt, and Oliver reported on the 27th only the usual vain confidence in the friendship of the soldiers when the blow was struck. [P13; P14] On the night of the 9th people tended to come out into the streets on the strength of rumours that something was going to happen, but the nearest Nottingham came to joining in the insurrection was the gathering of perhaps a hundred people in Nottingham Forest, some with pikes and some with poles, who hung around for a short time and then dispersed without any need for official action. Trivial as this was, and it was hardly sufficient to warrant the Under-Sheriff's description of 'a very large assemblage', it was sufficient for the crown solicitor, Lockett, to advise the Home Secretary that it constituted the insurrectionary demonstration at Nottingham which the Pentrich rebels had expected and was proof of the premeditated nature of the rising. But by Nottingham standards it was a pathetic showing, and the men dispersed quietly without causing any inconvenience. [P44; P14; P16]

Of the rebel army itself it is very difficult to form a precise estimate. Forty-five prisoners were later indicted for their part, 'together with a great multitude of false traitors . . . unknown to the number of five hundred and more arranged and armed in a warlike manner'. How this number of perhaps 550 was arrived at is not known. During the course of William Turner's trial, a witness, Henry Hole, attempted to estimate the size of the various contingents and reckoned that their total was somewhere over 300. [P44] Cobbett's account suggested that the total did not exceed 200, and the Hammonds, ready enough to discount the importance of the revolutionary strand in working-class history, suggested that probably fewer than 200 joined the insurrection. [P59; s23, 361] If allowance is made for the pressing and coercion of men, it is clear that the Pentrich rebels were far from being the people in arms. Instead of adding to their strength as they passed through more villages, they tended to lose recruits as opportunities for escape presented themselves, and wherever they passed they provoked fear and condemnation, not rejoicing. By the time the rebels were officially spotted near Eastwood they were 'not very numerous' and able to be tackled, in Under-Sheriff Leeson's words, by two of the County magistrates 'at the head of a few Dragoons'. [P13] The behaviour of the country people as a whole was such as to win them plaudits from both the Duke of Newcastle and the Home Secretary, and Rolleston happily reported that the country people had been violently opposed to the rebel force. [P13] Later in the month the Duke of Devonshire was sent news that Derbyshire, like the rest of the country, was in a tranquil state, as it had been, with the exception of a very few villages, on the night of 9 June. [P2] The whole conspiracy, as the defence solicitors were to suggest to counsel, was confined to small numbers of persons and was of such a nature that the laws of the country afforded ample means for taking care of it. [P2] That the government chose to give the rebellion special treatment was a matter of political decision and not of legal necessity.

And if the rebel army was small in numbers and lacking popular backing, it was hardly a well-equipped fighting force either. The rebellion was not preceded by fairly systematic arms thefts, and there were no extensive caches of weapons known to be available when the call came. It was certainly asserted that three men had been engaged at Pentrich in the manufacture of pikes for a period of three weeks before the rebellion, and these were presumably the weapons described by Under-Sheriff Leeson in his letter of 10 June to Newcastle; they had, he said, at the Nottingham police office a dozen of the rebels' forks and pikes, the latter 'manufactured out of old files or chisels sharpened affixed to handles of considerable length'. [P12; P13] The conspirators seem to have relied more on the expectation, or at least the hope, that somehow they would acquire arms from the military establishment in the area, and much of their discussion, as reported by spies, concerned the means by which they were to dispossess the soldiers, either by visiting the local public houses where they were stationed or by attacking the points where arms were believed to be stored. It was believed, for instance, that there were 100 stand of arms at Wollaton, but plans for their acquisition were hardly matured when Abraham Smith, a former private in the Nottingham Fencibles, notified the Town Clerk that the conspirators had asked him the way to Lord Middleton's house there, betraying a surprising ignorance of local topography for men preparing to take over the nation. [P16] Individuals were expected to show some initiative in arming themselves, and another spy reported on 25 May that those unable to obtain fire-arms had been instructed to acquire a pole some eight or nine feet in length with a spike at the end of it. 'Spike' rather than 'pike' was in fact the local generic term for this kind of weapon, which compelled members of the bench to seek occasional elucidation at the subsequent trials.

The arms of the marching army consisted then of some guns, pikes and even forks, the last adding to the illusion of a peasants' revolt, and their principal hope on the night of the rebellion must have been in the weapons they could commandeer on the way or acquire from a friendly soldiery in Nottingham and perhaps in the arsenal that Butterley iron-works would soon become in their possession. Whether, as John Cope, an employee there, a conspirator who turned King's evidence, informed them, Butterley was capable of turning out five cannon and 300–400 pikes per day, whether the rebels would have the technical know-how, and the iron-works the flexibility, to permit this immediate conversion to military production, and whether this would have made a significant contribution to the needs of a rebel army, must all remain unanswered questions. [P16] Though the rebels exchanged words with those on guard at Butterley, they did little more, and the absence of any serious attempt to take the works suggests that it did not feature prominently in the rebel scheme and was perhaps just one more hazy idea of what might be done to help promote revolution. It probably seemed an appropriate thing to try to do, if all the right things were to be done, but no one had given more careful thought to how the iron-works was to be taken over than to the problem of how the resources of the army were to find their way into rebel hands. And so Pentrich was an affair of pikes and forks, and on the occasion when a gun was fired it killed not a tyrant in high places but a farm servant, by accident.

Rebellions are made by rebels, and the strength of a movement is no greater than that of its members, in the case of so ambitious yet so tiny a movement, perhaps, no greater than that of its leaders. William Cobbett, in his American exile, stressed that the three executed leaders appeared to have been religious men, sober, thoughtful, beloved of all who knew them, who wept for their relations and friends, and who, in spite of their religious commitments, would not acknowledge that they had been wrong in what they had undertaken. [P59] It is doubtful if the young men and their families hounded from their beds by Brandreth on the night of 9 June would have subscribed to this view of him. Distance lent enchantment to Cobbett's vision: the behaviour of the government and the pathetic stories concerning the men and their families in their last days ensured for them a very sympathetic treatment from the radical press in their own time and earned for them an elevation to the ranks of those of 'heroic stature' in later days. Yet such tributes have perhaps been paid a little indiscriminately. [s57, 648]

Of Jeremiah Brandreth little is known though much has been inferred. When judgment was passed upon him he was described as a well-known figure, but the investigations of the Nottingham Journal uncovered practically nothing. [P66] He was believed to be twenty-seven years old, of Irish or gipsy extraction, though perhaps born in Exeter and possessing a Dutch family name. He had reputedly worked as a drover, a whitesmith, a sailor, and a stocking-maker in his time, was thought to have been a Luddite, a usual assumption made about all radicals in this area, and he and his family had been recently removed to Wilford, according to the parish overseer, from Sutton-in-Ashfield, where he had been an unemployed stockinger. [s36, 94; P63] He was believed to have acquired a little education, sufficient to give him some status with his fellow workers, but the illiterate communication of 19 May, in which he invited Henry Enfield's spy to attend a meeting at his house, speaks less for his attainments than the widely cited correspondence with his wife. [P16]

Also, it would appear from testimony at the trial that the confusion about the meaning of 'provisional government' was Brandreth's, not that of one of his followers, unless this was a deliberate ploy to attract support. [P44] No one from Pentrich appears to have had prior acquaintance with him, and during the rebellion itself he was known only by his title of 'The Nottingham Captain' and not by his name. He appears to have worked hard during his four days in Derbyshire, and such a rebellion as took place on 9 June was his doing. He has been described on the one hand as an 'experienced revolutionary', on the other as a 'traditional rebel . . . a stalwart, desperate fellow . . . old-fashioned to the point of reaction'. [s57, *733*; s65, *168*]

The other three men capitally convicted for their part in the Pentrich Rebellion are remarkable only in the blameless and undistinguished lives which they appear to have lived before their one moment of notoriety when all their respectable past was set at nought. No one knew Brandreth and no one could say anything about him. Everyone knew William Turner, a stonemason by trade, Isaac Ludlam, a labourer who had known better days in business, and George Weightman, a sawyer, yet no one seems to have had the least suspicion of the fate to which they were heading. The making of rebels from men of good character and peaceable disposition is a process that cannot be described and can only be inferred. Their followers were representative of all groups in the local community, mainly described as labourers, though many so described were probably framework-knitters. In addition there were quarryworkers and stonemasons, and men from other country occupations, farmers, blacksmiths, sawyers, even a tailor. [s36, *39–40*]

The professional revolutionary in the midst of these men was not Jerry Brandreth but Thomas Bacon, professional in the sense that organising revolutions was practically a career with him until his last-minute withdrawal from the plot, which might well have saved his life, though it was much too late to preserve his innocence. A framework-knitter by occupation, he was previously an iron-dresser at Butterley, though his role as the political thinker of the area would have gone well with a cobbler's craft; Bacon was not unlike John Baines, the Halifax hatter transported for allegedly administering illegal oaths in 1812, a veteran Jacobin of Tom Paine's day who took renewed hope of seeing his views implemented as each crisis approached and who was willing to modify his methods to meet the mood of the times. In the autumn and winter of 1816–17 he had been a Hampden Club man; by the spring he was a revolutionary, though he still professed to be pursuing the same basic aims of manhood suffrage and annual parliaments. He is said to

have advocated the equalisation of property, the break-up of great
estates, and the allocation of a few acres to each man. [s57, *722*] Born
into an industrial context a few years later, he would have been a
Socialist, for his radicalism appears to have embraced social as well as
political equality. 'It was owing entirely to his never-ceasing exertions
that the lower classes of the people in and around Pentrich have been
corrupted and seduced from their allegiance', and when the town clerk
of Nottingham established a look-out near Pentrich on 9 June it was to
watch 'the result of old Bacon's threatened movements', for Thomas
Bacon was thought to be the man mainly responsible for the Pentrich
Rebellion. [p20; s57, *722*]

He was certainly an incorrigible traveller and the epitome of the
itinerant delegate who did so much among the radicals of the day to
foster the illusion that they possessed strength and organisation because
of the existence of a few personal contacts between one place and another.
Cobbett and Bamford remembered him as one of the Hampden Club
deputies from the London conference in January 1817, but when conspiracy was in the air in April he was off again, apparently taking with
him £1 of his brother John's rent-money on the grounds that the business
on which he was engaged was more important than paying the rent. [p59;
p16] His important venue was Wakefield and his meeting with Oliver,
but before that he had visited Lancashire, for Samuel Bamford encountered at the 'Dog and Partridge', Middleton, this familiar figure of
'an aged grey-headed man, stooping beneath probably seventy years,
his venerable locks hanging to his shoulders, and having in one hand a
stick, and on the other arm a basket containing rolls of worsted and
woollen yarn, and small articles of hosiery which he seemed to have for
sale'. He told Bamford of the delegate meeting to be held in Yorkshire
and of the 'finishing blow to be levelled at the borough-mongers'. This
sounded to Bamford too much like the rest of the revolutionary plots
that were regularly being proposed to him, and he would have nothing
to do with Bacon's scheme. [p28]

After this he was everywhere, trips to Yorkshire, over to Leicester,
and frequently to Nottingham, and informers' accounts of meetings they
had attended invariably contained some reference to the presence of 'the
old man'. Enfield's spies notified him of Bacon's presence at a meeting
in Nottingham on 23 May and reported the taking of a collection to
finance a trip to Manchester, while Oliver himself duly reported the
presence of 'Old Bacon the original Nottingham delegate' at Manchester
on 31 May. [p16; p14] According to the Crown solicitors he had been in
all the disaffected towns and had contacts there; he was known through-

out radical company in the North and the Midlands and, like Oliver himself, supplied one of the vital links that suggested to the conspirators that they were a nationally connected and organised force. [P20] In addition he still appeared frequently in his own village of Pentrich to spread the good news and persuade his neighbours of the need to prepare themselves. Although Bacon withdrew from the conspiracy at the last moment this was not sufficient to save him from the law, and his name was to appear at the head of all the others in the indictment of prisoners later on trial, a clear indication of the role he was believed to have played in the making of the Pentrich Rebellion.

But if the government believed, or professed to believe, that Thomas Bacon was the instigator of the June rebellion, it quickly became a fundamental article of radical faith that the rebellion had been the doing of Oliver the Spy, employed by Sidmouth, according to Cobbett, to justify the false charges which were currently being made against the press and against reformers, to justify the retention of repressive legislation, and to prepare the way for the total destruction of freedom of the press. [P59] This kind of interpretation, which has remained the popular view of the events of this time, may or may not exaggerate the degree of malice in the Home Secretary's motivation, but it clearly exaggerates his capacity to devise and control so elaborate an enterprise. This was no systematic operation since system is so evidently lacking, and the extent of Oliver's success arose from a combination of good fortune and the peculiar abilities of the man who happened to present himself for a job which happened to occur to him.

On 28 March Oliver arrived at the Home Office seeking employment for such talents as he possessed, and by 24 April he had a sufficiently formulated plan and the necessary associates to carry it through to secure Sidmouth's approval for his proposed roving commission among extreme radicals and reformers, where he would pick up intelligence of conspiracies against the government of the day. [P14] He was more concerned to establish his credentials with the 'reformers' than with the authorities on this first trip, and his enterprise was known only to his employer. Before his second trip Sidmouth sent out a covering letter of 22 May concerning this 'person well acquainted with the designs of the disaffected . . . an intelligent man, and deserving of your confidence', but the distribution of the letter was somewhat random. [P16] As a result the commander-in-chief in the West Riding apparently knew nothing of him before the end of May, and Oliver almost came to grief at the hands of Sheffield magistrates on 29 May. [s23, *355–7*]

Sidmouth's success with Oliver arose from good luck rather than good

management, and it was fortunate for him that some local authorities
maintained a much more efficient intelligence system than he could
command. Nottingham, in particular, with its vast experience of illegal
enterprises during Luddite years, was well provided for in this respect,
and the town clerk was able to supply the Home Secretary with detailed
accounts of conspirators' meetings for three weeks before the rebellion
took place and had been able to give assurance that all was known about
and under control even before that period.

Yet Oliver was the man who visited and reported on all the centres
and who supplied the overall picture, and it is important that his role in
the rebellion should be elucidated. Of his character it might seem
sufficient to say that the nature of his employment required that he
should be an accomplished liar and that there are many indications from
his earlier life that he was admirably qualified in this respect. His relevant
experience, according to those who took the trouble to find out, and
these probably did not include his employer, included bigamy, fraud
against a former employer and a spell in a debtors' prison, but these
experiences he survived to become Bamford's 'well-dressed and apparently affluent stranger' and Bacon's 'man of Fashion', who stood out
among his fellows at the Wakefield meeting of 5 May. [P63; P28; P14]
Such was the man on whom so much depended; on the one hand the
prospects of the rebels to assess their own strength, on the other the
ability of the government to assess the danger in which it stood.

The travels of Oliver have been described on several occasions, and
apart from minor discrepancies over dates, which arise in part because
of Oliver's tendency to leave some places and arrive at others during the
night, there is little disagreement over his timetable. That arises over the
words he spoke and the part he acted at his various stopping places, and
unfortunately for the historian this subject is one of those on which there
is no such thing as untainted evidence. Everyone who contributed to the
argument was an interested party, and the partial statements of one side
can only be balanced against the partial statements of the other.

Those who sought to label Oliver as an *agent provocateur* included
those who had themselves been involved in the conspiracy and who were
presumably anxious to lessen their own guilt and emphasise the mischief
of the government agent. They also included the government's radical
critics in parliament, defence counsel Thomas Denman, and William
Cobbett, the journalist. A last impeachment of Oliver came from his
fellow spy Bradley, who claimed to have been present when Sidmouth
criticised Oliver for going too far in his proceedings, 'at which Oliver
was all of a tremble', but one spy's comments on the performances of

another might reasonably be supposed the most tainted of all sources. [P12]

The government and Oliver himself took a different view of the whole affair. According to Oliver, at the famous Wakefield meeting he simply noted down, without encouraging, what information and ideas the others brought forward, and his function was to encourage confidences by subtle hint and suggestion, by nods and winks, by listening to the boasts of others without attempting to contradict them, by conveying an impression of knowledge, and of enthusiasm, without actually committing himself to precise words, and to allow others to deceive themselves by a non-committal response rather than deliberately to encourage or mislead them by positive statements. [P14] There is only Oliver's word to support these claims about his actual statements at meetings; all other people who attended them formed a different impression, but they were intended to do so. In the final analysis there is no means of knowing what Oliver really said to his audiences, only the general impression with which he left them, and the inferences which they drew from his presence wherever he went were invariably that London and other parts of the provinces were strongly for revolt and that it was up to his audience of the moment not to fall behind the rest.

Certain tentative conclusions might be offered about Oliver and his role. That groups of militants existed before Oliver appeared on the scene is quite clear; he did not create revolutionaries out of nothing, though he probably encouraged them both by what he said and what he did not say. Nor was he responsible for the notion of an armed insurrection, for that too had preceded Oliver, though he probably contributed more to the shaping and formulation of the insurrection that finally took place in June than he was ever prepared to admit. His connections with Brandreth are very tenuous and difficult to establish. A meeting between the two men has never been proved, and Brandreth went off to Pentrich on the 5th, in advance of Oliver's final arrival in Nottingham during the night of 6/7 June. Despite growing suspicions that Oliver was a spy and that his promises, such as they were, were not to be relied upon, Brandreth was not recalled and the rebellion went ahead, even if the Nottingham associates had learned enough personally to desist from rebellion or even to flee the country. The determination of some men to proceed with rebellion, whatever Oliver's position, and the technical impossibilities of bringing home to Oliver's door precise responsibility for the events of 9 June, have probably resulted in the spy being judged much too lightly in recent years. [s54, 204–6] It is not satisfactory to attempt to draw a clear line between the activities of informer and *provocateur*, for anyone successfully practising the arts of the one must almost inevitably descend to the deceptions of the other. Whatever Oliver's actual words to the companies among whom he moved, he conveyed an impression, whether by his speeches or his silences, that revolution was going ahead throughout the country and was himself understood to be the sign that there was a national leadership in London which expected revolution and was prepared to give it direction. Exactly how Oliver managed to convey this impression is more academic than important, but his villainous reputation within traditional Whig historiography remains largely undamaged.

With Oliver safely back in London, and the rebellion safely put down, it remained but to pursue those men who had not been caught by Rolleston's party on the morning of 10 June, and to ensure that the leaders were convicted of their crime of high treason and waging war upon the King, for a lesser charge of riotous assembly or affray would clearly not satisfy those who had known for so long that rebellion was to occur and who had taken no steps to prevent it. On 26 July forty-five prisoners were indicted at Derby Assizes on three counts of high treason, the first being that of 'levying war against His Majesty, involving arming themselves and marching through the countryside in hostile array', and on 16 October a Special Commission at Derby began to try the case of Jeremiah Brandreth.

The trials of Brandreth, Turner, Ludlam and Weightman make curious reading in that they present the Pentrich Rebellion in isolation, as something that was almost conceived and executed in less than forty-eight hours rather than as the culmination of more than two months' activity. Basing their case against the four men on the one meeting and the rebellion alone, the prosecution had a pathetically easy task of proving the charge of treason against the defendants and could do so without any need to refer to the previous build-up which might have taken them into the more dangerous territory that Oliver had frequented, to the knowledge of all who had heard of the disclosures of the *Leeds Mercury* and the embarrassment they had caused the government. [P63]

With the capital conviction of the four men who had been most prominent on the night of 9 June the government evidently felt that enough had been achieved. According to a letter from one of the presiding judges to the Home Secretary on 1 November a deal was evidently arrived at between the attorney-general and defence counsel by which the remaining prisoners were persuaded to change their plea to 'guilty' on the understanding that their lives would be spared. [P16] Twelve were allowed to go free on account of their age, while the rest were sentenced to varying periods of transportation. Among these was Thomas Bacon, the man the authorities were most determined to convict. But Bacon, though named first in the indictment on all counts, could not have been proceeded against for waging war against the King, arming himself and marching through the countryside in hostile array, since he did none of these things; he could be charged only under the second count of the indictment for meeting 'to devise, arrange, and mature plans and measures to subvert and destroy the Constitution'. Bacon had been present at neither the 'White Horse' meeting of 8 June nor the rebellion of 9 June, and so the case successfully mounted by the Crown against the four leaders would not have served the purpose against Bacon. In fact it is questionable if they could have mounted any case with any reasonable hope of success. Against Bacon the Crown had no one and nothing else to confirm the testimony of accomplices; no papers had been found on Bacon, he had not been seen going to or returning from meetings, he had made no confession of his activities to examining magistrates, and he had not joined in the rebellion. The prosecution was desperate to have Bacon convicted because of his known instigating role in the conspiracy, but lacked the means of securing the conviction. It seems not improbable that Thomas Bacon's transportation was the price paid for the lives of his fellow prisoners, and that his lawyers assumed personal responsibility for the decision and were not altogether unsympathetic to the Crown's view that Thomas Bacon had been foremost among the conspirators.

On the morning of 7 November Jeremiah Brandreth, William Turner and Isaac Ludlam were hanged at Derby for high treason, George Weightman's sentence having been commuted. Their sentence, wrote Thomas Bacon while awaiting transportation, was too severe; men of Yorkshire and Lancashire, apprehended on similar charges, had been liberated, and one offence during the passage through life ought to be forgiven. Nor had it previously been known, he wrote, for men of this humble station to be tried for high treason, 'men who can scarce tell a letter in the alphabet'. [P14] There were many who agreed with him and many more who were repelled by disclosures about government methods of espionage. The fate of the revolutionaries seems to have brought moderates and extremists closer together rather than driven them further apart, as the government remained unrepentantly opposed to reform, and its upholders, such as the Duke of Newcastle, responded to protest by issuing declarations concerning the 'blessings of such an enviable and excellent Constitution' to be encountered in no other country on earth. [P13]

3 The Union Societies, Peterloo, and the Scottish Radicals

In the three years after Pentrich the trends and tendencies of the previous thirty reached their climax. The reformers demonstrated beyond doubt their capacity to create and lead, if only for a short time, a popular movement which sought remedies for multifarious economic discontents in the reform of parliament. Those in authority demonstrated yet again their unwillingness to accommodate this movement and their misunderstanding of the aims and the methods of their critics. And those who were the targets of government repression demonstrated once more that revolution is attempted when reform movements are stifled. The years 1817–20 followed a familiar, almost predictable, pattern, but it was the last time the pattern would appear. Future governments would never again adopt quite such negative and short-sighted policies and reformers in the future would never again be driven to insurrection by the total frustration that had confronted their predecessors. Nor would the cause of political reform retain the popular allegiance that it appeared to have in 1819 as the grand panacea for all discontents; the working classes would identify all kinds of legitimate aspirations requiring satisfaction, and campaigning for the franchise would be only one, and not necessarily the most important, activity to occupy their attentions and energies in the future. Popular movements would become increasingly organised, but not necessarily concerned with political reform.

After the abortive rebellion of June 1817 rumours of plots and revolt subsided, though the reformers found in the spy issue another grievance on which to voice their dissatisfaction. Habeas corpus came into force again at the beginning of 1818, and in July the Seditious Meetings Act lapsed. The way was clear for the reform movement to reorganise, and the initiative came from the weavers of the North-West, who were continuing to experience falling wages that could not be stabilised by strikes and industrial organisation. In place of the defunct Hampden Clubs there appeared union societies, modelled partly on the organisation of the clubs and accepting an educational role 'for the purpose of acquiring and diffusing political information' among working men. The first society was founded in Stockport with an organisational framework laid down by a radical nonconformist preacher and owing much to the Methodist class system. Stockport was divided into twelve sections, each subdivided into classes of twelve, and it became the pattern for numerous similar societies which were formed throughout the North as economic conditions worsened in the winter of 1818–19. [s41, *47–50*] Stockport also gave the lead to the English Midlands and western Scotland, for these too were among the disturbed areas of the country in 1819. It was an English radical, Joseph Brayshaw, who introduced union societies into the cotton-weaving areas around Glasgow 'to extend political knowledge and the sentiment of Reform'. The Scottish union societies were 'composed of from twelve to fifteen or twenty Radical Reformers in the district – one out of each of these commonly called a Class leader constituted a meeting called the Committee of the district, and one or more Delegates from the District formed the Central Committee which met once a week in Glasgow'. Funds came from members' subscriptions. They helped to purchase 'the most seditious and treasonable publications' which, according to Lord Advocate Rae, 'the best educated read to the rest'. [P22; P69; P52] Amid deepening economic depression in 1819, the societies moved on from political education to a revival of mass meetings, and in June radicals in both Manchester and Glasgow took over open-air meetings that had been called to petition for state-aided emigration and diverted them into demands for parliamentary reform. There was an open-air meeting called in Glasgow to consider 'the distressed state of the country and the necessity of a Reform in the Commons House of Parliament' three days before the widely heralded assembly that was to take place on St Peter's Fields, Manchester, on 16 August. [P22]

The Manchester meeting, along with rallies in London, Leeds, and Birmingham, was part of a more aggressive campaign to demonstrate to the government the great popular support that the radicals could now mobilise, support that was to be expressed in 'remonstrances' to the Prince Regent rather than the traditional, more humbling tactic of petitioning. This phase of the reform movement, culminating in Peterloo, illustrates supremely well the readiness of the authorities to confuse reform with revolution. Its aftermath illustrates both the vulnerability of reform movements to the designs of extremists and the way in which governments could make revolutionaries out of reformers by their own policies.

There is no doubt that radical reform had made greater headway among greater numbers of people in Lancashire in 1819 than it had ever done before. The proliferation of union societies, the mass meetings which they organised, the large numbers they were mobilising behind a radical programme of manhood suffrage, annual parliaments, and Corn Law repeal, and the growth of a radical press, all these betokened a degree of activity not previously known. [s42, 56] And if the language of their speakers was sometimes undisciplined, the rank and file were acquiring the habit of orderly marching behind banners, which they practised in open drilling sessions in an attempt to ensure discipline in their appearance and behaviour.

But there was an ambiguity about all their activities. On the one hand it has been demonstrated that the reformers were advocating a peacable programme of reform; at the same time it has been shown how their methods inspired a belief that they were planning a revolution. The mass meetings were thought to be agitating the public mind in preparation for insurrection; the pikes and the sticks of the reformers were brought to meetings not for protection but in readiness for insurrection; the drilling was not for self-discipline but for action. The Manchester authorities expected people to come armed to the meeting of 16 August, and when they arrived in such enormous numbers and displaying such a degree of organisation the magistrates 'felt a decided conviction that the whole bore the appearance of insurrection'. And so they sent in the yeomen cavalry with such disastrous consequences.

It is significant that a recent, highly detailed attempt to clear the magistrates of the blame and odium traditionally attached to them for their handling of affairs has made no attempt 'to prove that the radicals were following revolutionary courses', only to suggest that their language and actions not surprisingly suggested to the magistrates that this was their intent. [s60, 71] In other words, the vindication open to the magistrates, that they stopped a revolution, has not been established, nor even attempted, and the argument continues to concern whether or not they acted reasonably in interpreting circumstances that were ambiguous. Indeed, it is conceded that the authorities were unable to make any discrimination between insurrectionary plotting and the open reform movement of 'correspondencies and systems of delegates', which their practitioners regarded as peaceful and constitutional methods of achieving reform and which historians have traditionally identified in similar terms. [s60, 103] If they believed that their activities were merely a cover for secret, revolutionary designs, and that Henry Hunt was planning to lead a revolution, their reputation stands or falls upon their judgment; and in the absence of any such proven conspiracy or even any

attempts to prove such, their reputation must remain essentially un-
changed even when their difficulties are recognised.

The reformers themselves were not, of course, unaware of the interpretation that would be placed upon their conduct. Hunt expressed his
regret that some working-class groups were playing at soldiers, and he
insisted that no one should come armed to Peterloo. The whole idea of
mass meetings had been denounced by the *Manchester Gazette* shortly
before Peterloo on the grounds that they merely gave the government
'an excuse for arbitrary measures'; it was in fact the mass meeting, or
rather the idea of simultaneous mass meetings of protest, that represented the main tactic of the ultra-radicals in the months after Peterloo,
a tactic that illustrates the escalation of protest after the violent suppression of a peaceful demonstration and the ability of extremists on the
fringes of the reform movement to acquire temporary ascendancy in this
kind of situation. Lancashire was visited by Thistlewood and Watson,
who had earlier been involved in the Spa Fields riots and would later be
leaders of the Cato Street Conspiracy, and these committed revolutionaries helped to promote the new tactic of simultaneous mass meetings, which, it was hoped, might be the means of stimulating some sort
of general rising. The idea was vague in its intent and its implementation
unsuccessful, but it did for a time mark the conversion of some part of
the working-class reform movement to policies, or at least hopes, of
direct action as an outcome of political protest, and in December 1819
brought Manchester to another very tense situation. In the event the
Lancashire reform societies quickly collapsed as the government brought
in a new round of repressive legislation, the Six Acts. The extremists who
survived locally had no part in London's Cato Street Conspiracy, and
the weavers who had formed the popular basis of the political movement
showed, not for the last time, the unreliability of their political alle-
giances by allowing a temporary improvement in their prosperity to turn
them away from politics. [s42, *160–1*]

In the west of Scotland a similar story was to have a different kind of
ending. References to 'murderous carnage', 'inhuman butcheries', and
'tyrannical transactions' were made as people were enjoined to 'Remem-
ber Manchester' at mass meetings. Barely two months after the event,
Peterloo was already being depicted on a Rutherglen banner as 'a
woman, with a child in her arms, under the murderous sabre of a
Manchester yeoman...'. [p22; p69; p70] Peterloo and reform slogans
provided rallying symbols for thousands in the depressed Glasgow area,
where weavers looked to radical reform to rescue them from their
economic plight. Their meetings were peaceable and good tempered,

sometimes displaying the near-carnival spirit that had characterised Peterloo's early stages. Popular protest remained peaceful, and only when magistrates intervened, as they did at Paisley to seize a radical banner, did orderly crowds turn into rioting mobs and harmless people become menacing. It is likely (as a Hamilton lawyer, Robert Aiton, noted) that the huge crowds contained many who were idly curious and that the open-air rallies were a kind of public entertainment where singing and dancing added to the excitement offered by the dissemination of reform ideas. They certainly provided a useful safety valve so long as they were allowed to continue, though in Scotland too there were hopes that the union societies might be turned into rebel cadres and their mass meetings diverted from constitutional campaigning. [P22; P26]

As it became increasingly clear that the peaceful meetings had no hope of winning either reform or a Peterloo inquiry, a minority of extremists, with no well-laid plans for mobilising or co-ordinating armed groups, began to rest their hopes upon the calling of simultaneous mass meetings throughout the country as a signal and opportunity for armed groups to lead widespread rebellion. Alternatively, some believed that simultaneous rallies were simply an intensification of constitutional pressure, as evidenced by the resolution of a Paisley rally in September 'that the principal reformers in London be respectfully requested to meet and name a day for a simultaneous meeting of the reformers of the kingdom, in order to concert measures for reducing the powers of the borough-mongers'. [P52] This was the language of reformers, not revolutionaries, and the whole notion of simultaneous meetings remained thoroughly vague regarding organisation and aspiration. If actual insurrectionary conspiracy was the next stage of developments this was as much the doing of those in authority as of those in the radical vanguard. When Andrew Hardie embarked on high treason in April 1820 he did so because the other means open to him had both failed and ceased to exist. 'I went out', he was to write, 'with the intention to recover my rights . . . annual Parliaments and Election by Ballot . . . because I think Government ought to grant whatever the majority of the nation requested, and if they had paid attention to the people's lawful petitions the nation would not have been in the state . . . it was . . ..' [P43] Nor would Hardie have been in his current predicament, for he had become a revolutionary only when reform had failed, changing not his aims but only the means by which they were to be achieved.

One reason why the government chose to pursue repressive policies towards the reform movement during this period is that it was badly informed about its true nature, and one reason why it was badly informed is that, in the absence of any proper machinery for detecting the true state of affairs, it had to rely on the random offerings of spies, who were professionals only in the sense that they were paid for the intelligence which they supplied. The uncovering of the role of Oliver in the Pentrich Rebellion rendered the whole of government intelligence open to disbelief and has added since to the problem of elucidating the real nature of the threat that revolutionaries posed. Condemnations of Oliver and Sidmouth who employed him were intensified by the appearance of the spy John Castle as a witness at the London trial of some of the Spencean 'Spa Fields' conspirators, and by the outcry over Richmond the spy in Glasgow. Castle may well have been simply informing on the Spa Fields plot, but his appearance in court aroused the jury's suspicions of fabricated evidence and led to the collapse of the prosecution. Richmond was certainly guilty of inaccuracies and exaggerations and almost certainly of deliberately exacerbating the Glasgow oathing campaign. By contrast Oliver had supplied accurate and very useful information during his tours of spring 1817, though his efforts had clearly demonstrated the inability of the successful spy to avoid playing too the part of *provocateur*.

The government's problem was that it was increasingly being called upon to play a major role in the preservation of public order, which local authorities were increasingly unable to handle on their own. Industrialisation, urbanisation and internal migration were crowding a fast-growing population into the towns of the north of England or the greater Glasgow area and overtaxing the abilities of local magistrates to maintain their control. An Oliver or a Richmond was no part of any systematic attempt by the government to deal with the problem of law and order or even to implement a deliberately provocative policy, but rather were they temporary expedients, part of an unsystematic effort to cope with a crisis in administration and public order for which a long-term solution had yet to be devised.

Local magistrates, military leaders, prominent individuals and the Home Office acted independently, in only partial co-ordination, or even in a kind of sceptical rivalry. Spies spied upon more spies, and magistrates unwittingly arrested agents working for other magistrates or for the government. And when the reports were presented the authorities had the almost impossible task of deciding how much of them was to be trusted. Scotland's Lord Advocate told the Home Secretary:

The truth is that in Glasgow there is a most defective system of police. The Magistrates have in consequence no certain information of what the disorderly persons have at any time in view. They are obliged to trust in a great measure for information to individuals employed and paid for as spies at the moment. These persons are often very ill-informed themselves, and in order to make the information they give appear valuable they are but too apt to exaggerate the danger. [P55; s65, *107*; P22]

Unreliability stemmed from the incentive which payment-by-results gave to exaggeration, from informers being untrained in distinguishing between rumour and fact, between hopes and plans; and from the doubtful characters of the spies themselves, recruited from among debtors, convicts and opportunists. Some turned exaggeration into agitation and acted as *agents provocateurs*. Their machinations included the encouragement of the attack on Westhoughton steam-loom factory back in 1812, and the active instigation of some of the oathing ceremonies in the northern cotton towns. [s23, *350*; P28; s16, *182–3, 287*] It is not surprising that juries increasingly suspected all spies of being at best unreliable, at worst liars and *provocateurs*, and inclined to dismiss cases that rested upon spies' evidence. Nor is it surprising that those in government at national and local level should have had difficulty assessing the true extent of the revolutionary threat when they had to rely on such informants. But it would be as wrong to suppose that all they reported was false as it would to suppose that it was all true. Nor is it possible to accept uncritically the allegations of those reformers who maintained that all insurrectionary conspiracies were the work of *agents provocateurs*.

Another reason why the government was repressive was that a reform movement that had one purpose to its members, and that a perfectly legitimate one, had a totally different one in the eyes of its critics. What to the radical reformers was a reasonable demand for manhood suffrage was a thoroughly unreasonable and subversive proposal to those not in sympathy with the demand. What was political information and education for the radicals was sedition and blasphemy to the authorities. When the radicals attended their mass meetings towards the end of 1819 armed with sticks which they said were for defending themselves against un-provoked attack such as had occurred at Peterloo, the authorities feared that they were for the purpose of turning meetings into uprisings. And when the Earl of Glasgow noted the 'military precision, silence, and order' of several thousand people marching to a meeting near Paisley, he did not rejoice in their peaceable conduct but noted darkly that

> while the Reformers of this district call out 'Order' at their meetings, and can systematically preserve it when it suits their policy or humour,

their public harangues are of the most *audacious* and Revolutionary description. The expectation of a subversion of the Government is so deeply rooted in their minds, that whenever a leader shall arise, or a favourable moment occur, I fear a considerable proportion of the population could not be depended upon.

On this occasion the Lord Advocate – relying on information from military leaders, magistrates and his own spymaster, Captain Brown – reported that the Earl was 'under a degree of apprehension for which there does not appear . . . to be any adequate cause'. [P22]

The reality was always difficult to separate from the fears. When simultaneous mass meetings were being planned in November 1819, the three senior Scottish law lords 'were all quite satisfied that it will come to blows, and that speedily'. Reports that ultra-radicals in Manchester and Glasgow were planning meetings for 13 December heightened fears of revolution, and on 11 December parliament passed the first of Sidmouth's Six Acts, against private drilling and armed training, and troop movements began around Manchester and Glasgow. [P9; S42, *157*] In neither place was there any attempt at revolt. The only activity in Glasgow was a gathering of radicals at Pollokshaws addressed by a shoemaker, and Major-General Sir Thomas Bradford rationalised the non-occurrence of revolt as the result of the union societies' abandoning their plans on learning of the troop movements. The non-event demonstrated to him the success of his precautions rather than the groundless nature of his fears. The streets remained quiet, and his yeomanry, troops and artillery were gazed at with amazement and incredulity rather than treated to the hostility which Bradford's interpretation should have produced. [P69; P22; P9]

For all the apparent calm the government was set upon a collision course. Premature congratulations of the magistrates and yeomanry responsible for Peterloo and subsequent refusals to hold an inquiry into the episode simply exacerbated a popular anger that vented itself from August to December in mass rallies. By December the government's alarm had led to a renewed bout of repression, with the restricting of mass meetings and the gagging of the radical press under Sidmouth's Six Acts. 'I have never known a period', wrote Henry Cockburn later, 'at which the people's hatred of the Government was so general and so fierce', and his experience covered the years 1779–1854. 'Prevalent distress among the lower orders was at the root of this, but the feeling was exasperated by the new and severe laws made for preventing popular meetings and punishing popular excesses . . . .' [P34] The consequence of the Six Acts of December 1819 was that the union societies, which had acted as organisers of open outlets for social unrest and discontent, were forced to disband or go underground. Revolt, which the reformers blamed on the spies and the government blamed on the reformers, was once more the consequence of repressive legislation which closed off lawful channels of open protest.

It is an understandable tactic that critics of the government should have tried to put the blame for plots, rebellion and revolutionary talk on to the spies, but it was an exaggerated view, like the government's own exaggeration of isolated plots into a widespread conspiracy. The real position lay somewhere between these two extremes. In the years 1817-20 there were undoubtedly advocates of rebellion at work in London, the East Midlands, Lancashire, the West Riding and the Glasgow area, largely artisans and unskilled workers and few in number. Their plots and oathings were not part of a national scheme of revolt, except when a Joseph Mitchell or an Oliver might create a superficial impression of co-ordinated activity. They were local, barely organised, virtually stillborn affairs, with only the vaguest notions of how they might attract support. Spies reported on local rebel talk and hopes and on rudimentary organisations that already existed, sometimes accurately, in the case of Oliver in the East Midlands, sometimes exaggeratedly, as in the case of Alexander Richmond in Glasgow. Undoubtedly there were always some militants ready to talk revolution with or without the prompting of spies, and in times of repression these men acquired a greater ascendancy and at the same time became the targets of the informers and *provocateurs*. After the break-up of the Hampden Clubs in 1817, according to Samuel Bamford, 'the people, at a loss to distinguish friends from enemies, were soon prepared for the operations of informers, who, in the natural career of their business, became also promoters of secret plots and criminal measures of various descriptions'. [P28] Difficulties in judging with certainty whether men who talked revolution were bona fide rebels or merely *provocateurs* were in themselves a deterrent against any large numbers of people risking involvement in a revolt that might be a trap. The penetration of spies was also a warning signal to the masses that whatever degree of rebel organisation existed locally, it was too weak and too vulnerable to betrayal once it attempted to establish links beyond its own district to permit successful revolt. The spies were invariably delegates from another community. With such prospects it was scarcely surprising that the vast majority held aloof from the conspiracies. Arrests, transportations and executions simply underlined the futility of revolt and reinforced the people's reluctance to rebel.

And yet, despite their experience and their prospects, there remained a few, even at the end of 1819, who were still ready to plot and conspire and set themselves up as targets for the informers and *provocateurs*. Some of the most determined were in Glasgow, even if that city presented an appearance of outward calm on 13 December to those soldiers who believed that they had forestalled rebellion by a show of strength on that day. According to one man later arrested as a radical 'delegate', military suspicions had not been unfounded; there had been an idea that the union societies should rise at this time but it had been cancelled, not on account of the display of force, but because no confirmation had arrived that a simultaneous rising would occur in England. [p22] If there ever was such an intention it is probable that it rested with just a few ultra-radicals in or close to Glasgow, for it is clear from the passive reactions of the local crowds that the would-be rebels had no links with the masses and had not stirred up any expectations of rebellion, let alone a readiness to join in. George Kinloch, a radical landowner arrested for addressing a mass meeting in Dundee, spoke for the west as well as the east of Scotland when he wrote to his wife on 12 December: 'I don't believe the people are so mad as to throw themselves on certain destruction . . ..' [s53, *164–5*] A few were, but unlike the reformers who had succeeded in rallying the masses in 1819, the physical-force militants were still showing no sign of being able to recruit large numbers to their cause. As Sidmouth clamped down on the press and the mass meetings of the open reform movement, repression spurred more men to join in talk of revolution but left the would-be revolutionaries still facing the problem of how to build organisational links to each other and to the masses.

It is known that a committee of radicals held weekly meetings in Glasgow towards the end of 1819 and contemplated joining England in a refusal to pay taxes after 1 January. It is not known how they obtained their information about the English intention, or why working-class radicals on both sides of the border should have opted for such a middle-class tactic of applying pressure, but this plan was superseded on 15 January by an agreement more appropriate to their social position, 'that there should be "a Strike" of work every where upon the first of March following and to continue for some days which it was thought would effectuate an Insurrection'. John McIntyre was delegated to go to Manchester to persuade the English radicals to rise too, and it was resolved that 'if England agreed' they should surprise the authorities by rising some days earlier. [p22] It is worth noting that Manchester was expected to speak for England, but one man sent from Glasgow was

hardly likely to elicit the necessary response. There had been no con-
certed effort and no activity either in December over political moves or
in January over the suggested tax strike, and contacts with England were
to remain weak, creating only an illusion of co-ordinated planning when
the reality was otherwise.

Nor had the Glasgow radicals established links within Scotland itself.
There is no evidence that they were in contact with Edinburgh or Dundee,
the other important industrial centre which had featured prominently
before this time, and neither the Highlands nor the Borders formed part
of their organisation save for a Dumfriesshire delegate amongst an
arrested group on 22 February. Even within the industrial west preparations for arming the people had not gone beyond the personal invitation
of individuals and a committee discussion of how radical ex-soldiers
might be called upon to provide drill and leadership. The forces to be
led were calculated quite unrealistically; 'there were ten thousand men
firmly united, well prepared and determined to go all lengths always
however in conjunction with England', and a further 20,000 were
thought to be willing to join the rebellion around Glasgow once it was
launched. Equally unrealistic was the supposition that insurrection
would receive the blessing of some Whig and Radical M.P.s who had
previously been sympathetic and would offer leadership once the ability
to command support had been demonstrated. This belief was an ever-
present part of the mythology of would-be revolutionaries over a long
period and helps to explain parliamentary fears of a rival assembly in the
making. In early 1820 the Glasgow committee of conspirators believed
that with this kind of backing 'a General Convention would probably be
formed so as . . . to organize a Government or Constitution upon
Radical Principles'. [p22]

At their meeting of 22 February the committee added a Carlisle
delegate, William Smith, to their number, but this move to strengthen
the English connection was little compensation for the news that emissary John Porter had brought back to Paisley, that no general rising was
being planned in England. And to complete their disarray their meeting
was raided by magistrates and troops and around thirty arrests were
made. Security measures had evidently been as defective as their attempts
at wider co-ordination, and they had fallen prey to an informer in their
own ranks. [p22; p52] The arrested men, said to be 'chiefly weavers and
cottonspinners', were from the towns and villages of the surrounding
area, 'a set of men who wanted to have a Radical Reform, Universal
Suffrage, and Annual Parliaments'. 'Part of their business', according
to Lord Provost Monteith, 'was to concert a plan of operation for the

beginning of March when a general rising was intended both here and in England . . .'. Some popular demonstration attended their imprisonment, and a sentry was said to have picked up a letter tossed from a cell window calling upon the populace to rise and liberate the prisoners. What became of them is not certain, but they were probably released on bail. [P22; P3; P9]

The Glasgow arrests almost coincided with the abortive Cato Street Conspiracy to assassinate the cabinet, and this prompted a Home Office aide, Hobhouse, to inquire if there was any connection between the two affairs. The Glasgow authorities replied that there was no evidence of collusion with London, and one of the arrested men swore that their links were not with the metropolitan radicals but those of Lancashire. These were certainly their aspirations, though it is possible, as Lanarkshire's sheriff depute, Robert Hamilton, surmised, that the Manchester radicals could have been in contact with both groups and made each aware of the other's intentions. [P55; P22] On the Manchester side, borough reeve Thomas Sharp claimed that a Scottish emissary had appeared in Manchester 'to warn the various Radical Sections, to hold themselves in readiness for the shortest notice, and . . . an explosion at no very distant period is contemplated'. This, together with the few scattered mentions of 1819–20 exchanges of radical contacts, shows that Glasgow area attempts at wider liaison were continuing to run along an axis to and from the cotton areas of northern England, as they had done in the 1812–13 Scottish cotton weavers' strike. [P3]

Despite the arrests a radical rump continued to meet around Glasgow, and one member, John Parkhill of Paisley, later recounted that 'it now began to be mooted, that the commencement of the resistance to the government was to take place on the first day of April, and that a proclamation was to be issued on that day . . .'. During March the north of England radical, Joseph Brayshaw, who had been in the Glasgow area in the summer of 1819 and had previously published 'An appeal to the people of England on the Necessity of Parliamentary Reform', was visiting radicals in Strathaven, Paisley and Parkhead village near Glasgow; and it was in Parkhead that the following proclamation was devised. A local magistrate, Thomas Hopkirk, reported after the affair that 'the sentiments in the Address were suggested by Brayshaw, when . . . he lived in James Armstrong's house, Parkhead, but these were put together by Robert Craig . . .'. Two printers with radical connections, John Hutchison and Robert Fulton, clandestinely printed the address at the premises of their employer in Saltmarket Street, Glasgow, and from a city alehouse 2000 copies were issued on 31 March and 1 April and distributed throughout the surrounding counties. [P22; P52; P62]

Unlike the magistrates of Nottinghamshire and Derbyshire in 1817, those of Glasgow were ill prepared in March 1820. They heard of the radical proclamation only just before its publication and had neither the time nor the manpower to stop it at source, prevent its distribution, or apprehend 'the disaffected, scattered over the towns and villages of five counties'. The central government was caught even more off guard. The lord advocate, the Home Secretary, the army commanders, all had heard nothing of the impending troubles. There was no preparedness at any level for the radical posters and placards that appeared over a wide area of Scotland's cotton-weaving west; even more shocking was the wide response to the call for a general strike from 1 April so that all could 'attend wholly to the recovery of their Rights'. The strike had run for twenty-four hours before the magistrates issued a counter-proclamation, and not until 29 April could they name the men wanted in connection with the address. [P22; P41; P62; P42]

The notion of a general strike as a means of launching a revolutionary uprising is a very interesting one. This was probably the first attempt in Britain at a general strike, albeit localised, and it had a political rather than industrial intent. There was apparently no thought of striking to bring the economic life of the nation to a halt, but rather to free men to attend to their political grievances, an idea that was to recur during Chartism. The west of Scotland weavers had shown remarkable solidarity in their industrial action of 1812–13 and this perhaps inspired the ideas of 1820, though on this occasion, unlike the former, there was no sign of organisational groundwork specifically for a strike. Instead there was a downing of tools and shuttles in response to the address, indication of spontaneous support or intimidation, according to viewpoint. Steps were certainly taken to bring the workers into line, for on the morning of 3 April in Glasgow 'most of the mills began work . . . but threatening visits were immediately paid to them, and the workers did not return at breakfast time, or have since left work'. A combination of persuasion and intimidation with spontaneous support appears to have brought virtually the whole of Glasgow's workers out on strike and to have halted work in neighbouring towns such as Paisley and Kilsyth. The strike did not extend beyond the economic orbit of Glasgow, but within that area it covered a wide range of towns, villages and trades, and had the support of weavers, cotton-spinners, colliers, machine-makers, ironfounders and wrights. It was, however, less easy to keep men out than to bring them out in such a time of economic distress. The strike began to collapse on the 5th, and by the 7th the weavers of Glasgow and Paisley were 'very generally returned to their looms', followed by the stragglers over the next few days. [P22; P62; P69; P60; P52]

Attempted co-ordination with Lancashire had been a failure. The borough reeve of Manchester was of the opinion that had the Scots held out for a week they would have been joined by men from his own area, but radical organisation had been inadequate to stage a simultaneous strike in Lancashire and possible sympathetic action can only be a matter for speculation. [P3] Scottish leaders were unable to capitalise on their own success, let alone mobilise other parts of the country, and popular anticipation of an organised rising under the 'Committee of Organisation for forming a Provisional Government', which had been foreshadowed by the Address, was not to be fulfilled. There proved to be no organisation capable of exploiting the initial unpreparedness of local and central government and turning a popular strike into a popular rebellion. A small-scale conspiracy was failing to produce a large-scale revolt.

Although the overwhelming majority of strikers did not take up arms it is worth noting that a few did. From various accounts of activity in Glasgow and its suburbs, in Paisley and Kilbarchan in Renfrewshire, Duntocher and Kirkintilloch in Dunbartonshire, and Balfron in Stirlingshire, it is clear that pikes were being made and arms stolen, and that men were drilling. From fragmentary evidence that exists and estimates offered, it might be calculated that the number of men possessing arms approached 1500, though of these less than 500 were reported as actually having paraded with weapons, a tiny minority of the working population and only a small part, it must be supposed, of the radicals in the area. [P22; P62; P60; P69; P52] And of those who paraded, two small ill-armed bands, acting in isolation and on impulse, were the only ones to translate their economic discontent and political convictions into open revolt. They were part of no overall plan and were misled by talk of reinforcements waiting to join them, by the mistaken expectation that the well-supported strike would bring thousands flocking to their ranks, and by the equally false hopes that England was up in arms.

Two small groups went beyond parading. About twenty men left Strathaven village for Glasgow on 5/6 April, under the leadership of a local veteran radical, James Wilson, only to flee into the night on discovering that the city was not in rebel hands. Meanwhile about forty rebels had set out from the Germiston district of Glasgow to raise support from the radicals of Stirlingshire, particularly those of Camelon and Falkirk who were among the labour force of the Carron ironworks.

The idea that they were planning to take over the ironworks to manufacture artillery was a much later addition to the story of which there is no contemporary mention; rather was it manpower which the rebels sought, with which they would return to Glasgow, where their comrades would, they hoped, already be in control.

In retrospect, pathetic abortive rebellions always seem unreal and the convictions of their leaders almost unintelligible. The leader of the group which left Glasgow for Stirlingshire was a young weaver, Andrew Hardie, deluded into the belief that revolution had come according to the pattern that had been talked about among the dreamers for several years: Glasgow was about to be up in arms, the non-arrival of the stage coach would indicate that England too had risen, the soldiers would offer no opposition, and the country waited to greet their arrival. In Condorrat, a weaving village some thirteen miles from Glasgow, a large party would join them, and an overall leader would assume command. This part, at least, of Hardie's beliefs was fulfilled, for John Baird, another weaver, awaited them at Condorrat with some pikeheads but only a handful of men. There were still encouraging tales told of a large number of armed men who were on their way from Glasgow, but more realistic was the intelligence of 'a man . . . from Camelon, who told that the people were unwilling to turn out . . . upon which went to the muir, determined to stay till night, when were to return to Glasgow'. Hardie was never able to carry out his revised plan, for an attempt to recruit the services of a lone Hussar, Sergeant Thomas Cook, resulted in that man's galloping off to Kilsyth to alarm his troops, who were resting there *en route* from Edinburgh to Glasgow. A small group of Hussars and yeomanry were sent in search of the rebels, and found Baird and Hardie's weary band resting on Bonnymuir, perhaps twenty-five strong and no formidable force. To the surprise of the soldiers, the rebels neither fled nor capitulated, but chose to stand their ground and fight armed only with '16 pikes, a shaft without a head, a gun or two, and two pistols'. There were wounded men on both sides, and eighteen prisoners were taken. [P43; P42; P69; P71; P22]

Bonnymuir and Strathaven were the futile gestures of tiny minorities, for the mass of the population had remained uninvolved. Glasgow had stayed free even of riot, though there was a violent demonstration against the military in Paisley and Kilsyth, and a jail attack in Greenock. In some Renfrewshire villages not guarded by soldiers people allegedly 'were seen openly preparing their arms for service – screwing the heads of their pikes into the shafts, cleaning their firearms etc. but still no actual violence took place'. These people were the second tier of the

April ferment of protest. There was a broad base of strikers, a much smaller group of stone throwers, arms raiders and preparers of pikes, and a tiny apex of rebels, the men who actually marched to revolution at Strathaven and Bonnymuir. From all this turmoil, only eighty-eight people had true bills of treason found against them, and not all these were accused of armed rebellion. About fifty-eight escaped capture, some by fleeing abroad. Thirty were tried, and between fifteen and twenty were transported to the Australian penal colonies, while James Wilson, John Baird and Andrew Hardie, the three leaders, were executed. [P22; P69]

There is no comprehensive list of the men arrested or indicted for high treason in the west of Scotland during 1820, but scanty and scattered sources for Stirlingshire, Ayrshire and Dunbartonshire suggest an occupational pattern for the rebels: it is possible to identify thirty-nine weavers, ten nailers, seven smiths, five cotton-spinners, three shoemakers and two tailors, as well as other crafts and occupations with single representatives. [P22; P62; P69; P71] Although the Rev. Thomas Chalmers, well known for his work and writing on Poor Law administration in Glasgow, believed that the leaders of the rebels were well-paid workmen in cotton and other factories, and that the higher paid cotton-spinners and colliers were just as radical as the deprived weavers, it appears to have been the domestic and workshop artisans, rather than the factory or mineworkers, who carried their disaffection to the point of rebellion. [s48, 108–9, 212; P69] Weavers made up the bulk of the mass meetings of 1819 and of the strikers and rebels, because they were the largest occupational group among West Scotland's industrial population and because their livelihood was in decline as well as in depression. Large numbers and a sense of threatened existence were peculiar to the weavers and explain their preponderance, but the presence of representatives of other trades indicates other factors, namely the distress of general depression and a wide political awareness sharpened by economic distress and the writings of the radicals, which seem to have been devoured with particular enthusiasm in the workshops, where there lingered a literacy achieved in better days. [s2, 46] And economic distress and political radicalism often appear to have been supplemented by military experience, for many of those who took up arms in April 1820 had served in the Napoleonic Wars and were young veterans still in their twenties and thirties, both experienced and disillusioned men. An over-simplified and faceless model would suggest that the man most likely to rebel in April 1820 was a young weaver or artisan who was also an ex-soldier imbued with radical ideas on politics and religion, and the known facts about the most prominent leaders support this broad picture. It would be interesting to have confirmation of a contemporary view that 'those who were the most distressed bore their sufferings without murmur'; it is clear that the leaders at least were men who were able to earn a living even in troubled times, while the 'very numerous, very poor' Irish immigrants, who were already coming into Glasgow in large numbers, added not one recognisably Irish name to the lists of indicted men. [P69; P23]

James Wilson, a stocking-weaver, the leader of the Strathaven men, was at sixty-three an exceptionally old rebel. He had a good reputation for his honesty and industry, despite the fact that his home 'was the place of general rendezvous for the disaffected for 25 years past . . .' where friends called to talk politics and read the radical papers. He had a long history of radicalism behind him. In 1792 he had joined the local group of 'Friends of the People', and when the more 'respectable' elements withdrew 'James Wilson, with some weavers and other mechanics of a speculative cast, came forward, held frequent meetings, and published new resolutions far more violent and irritating than those originally adopted . . .'. His dissident views were again evident during the weavers' strike of 1812–13, in the rise of the radical societies after 1815, and the union societies during 1819–20, when he was the Strathaven class leader. He housed Joseph Brayshaw during his visit to Scotland, and accompanied him to neighbouring towns and villages; he also helped to post up copies of the insurrectionary 'Address' before leading his own small contingent of rebels behind a union society banner on the abortive march into Glasgow. The inscription 'Scotland Free or a Desert' has allowed Wilson an unmerited reputation as an early nationalist, but his declared aim was to win reform, which he saw as 'the rights of their forefathers'. All his earlier political activity and his links with the English radical Brayshaw had been concerned with reform of the Westminster parliament, not with a Scottish breakaway from it, and Sir Francis Burdett himself acknowledged Wilson's part in the British reform struggle by a £10 gift to his widow. [P50; P32; P62; P69; P42]

John Baird, the leader of the Bonnymuir rebels, was also to declare that he had taken up arms to win reform and marched to Bonnymuir to win 'a radical reform of the Commons House of Parliament' and that he believed 'there was something of annual Parliaments in it'. He was thirty-one years old, and had fought in the Peninsular War. He too had a reputation within his village as a determined radical, and his pre-execution references to his pursuit of 'the cause of Truth and Justice' had a vague, idealistic content. Baird seems to have made the naïve assumption that the act of rebellion would be enough in itself somehow to compel a reform of parliament, but he did not appear to have thought out the mechanics of such a sequence or how political reform might lead to the economic betterment which he sought for working people. [P42; P69; P71]

Andrew Hardie, Baird's co-leader at Bonnymuir, was twenty-seven. He was deeply concerned with religious ideas and had given much thought to reconciling Christianity with rebellion, for he was firm in his belief that he was justified in taking up arms against Britain's 'higher powers'. 'Annual Parliaments and Election by Ballot' were his idea of the aims of the abortive rising, and these he had pursued through various reform activities and organisations in the post-war period, particularly his local union society. Like Baird, Hardie failed to explain how rebellion would achieve reform, but like him he believed that it would, and that better economic conditions would somehow follow. [P8; P42]

The absence of any realistic assessment by the leaders of their prospects of success, and their failure to think through the process by which rebellion might have led to reform, offer some slight support to the view advanced at the time and later that the Scottish rebels, like their English predecessors of 1817, were the victims of *agents provocateurs*. The documentary evidence does not support this view; nor do the known facts support the latest extravagant version of the *provocateur* thesis, that the rebels were Scottish nationalists who were led into a trap by the machinations of the Westminster government and its agents. [s19]

In the years 1812–20 Glasgow's political and economic situation had more in common with Manchester and north-western England than with the rest of Scotland. Glasgow's conditions and grievances were akin to those of the Lancashire cotton area, not to those of the thriving woollen and farming districts of the south-east borders, or of Edinburgh, or the Highlands with their peasant clearances. The west of Scotland radicals had acted in association with the English, or at least tried to do so, prior to 1820; they spoke not of a Scottish breakaway, but of reform within the overall British system, their proclamation was an 'Address to the Inhabitants of Great Britain and Ireland', and they hoped that their own rising was part of a general movement in which the English radicals were participating. The *Glasgow Herald* had suggested on 3 April that the address had been printed in England and that its reference to 'Magna Charta and the Bill of Rights', milestones for the English alone, indicated its English composition. Joseph Brayshaw was probably responsible for these references, though Magna Carta had already appeared on Scottish radical banners in 1819. Government papers clearly indicate that the 'Address' was the combined work of Brayshaw and some radical weavers in Parkhead village and that it was printed in Glasgow. [P62; P22]

Among the parliamentary radicals it was almost a matter of faith that government instigation lay behind all conspiracy, and Joseph Hume claimed to have proof of *provocateurs* at work in Glasgow since 1818. Castlereagh denied any government involvement, and the names mentioned by Hume do not feature either in the Scottish records or radical accounts of those years. [P62; P69; P22] And Scottish Whigs such as Henry Cockburn were no more successful in establishing their claim that 'there had been the secret agency of some in fomenting the treason'. [P69] The established authorship of the 'Address' clearly outweighs the conjectures that *provocateurs* were responsible, while the obvious unpreparedness of both local and central authorities undermines the thesis beyond redemption. This was no case of encouraging overt rebellion to make example, as Alexander Richmond, the former spy, was to claim; Richmond was party to neither radical nor official plans by 1819-20 and the rebellion had clearly caught the forces of law and order off guard. [P55; P22; P69] There had been no troops on hand to intercept the Strathaven marchers, and the Hussars alerted to the existence of the Bonnymuir rebels by their sergeant's chance encounter had arrived at Kilsyth only two hours before the intelligence reached them. A full twenty-four hours had elapsed between the posting up of the 'Address' and troop mobilisation, for the 80th Regiment and the 10th Hussars did not leave Edinburgh for the Glasgow area until 1 a.m. on 3 April. By this time the military and civil authorities were desperately trying to repair their fences and contain unrest, and not lying in wait to spring a trap prepared by *agents provocateurs*. [P62; P69; P71] Indeed, the April disturbances occurred at a time when both central and local authorities had allowed their espionage activities to lapse. In the absence of professional agents, the Glasgow magistrates picked up what they could from within the ranks of the radicals themselves, and had a notable success in the arrest of members of the radical committee on 22 February. Ironically the arrests reduced their capacity to maintain surveillance. As Lord Provost Monteith complained, 'we are not enabled now to procure that clear and satisfactory information that we have all along had, partly by some of our sources being lost by the arrestments, and chiefly by our not having the means of defraying the necessary expenses. We have no Corporation funds that can be applied for such purposes . . ..' Nor do government papers mention men alleged to have been spies though the existence of spies is well documented for earlier years. [P22]

Attempts have been made to argue that the Bonnymuir rebels had within their own number a certain John King, who had been retained by the authorities and who directed the soldiers to where the insurgents were resting. This alleged role is contradicted by reports of the subsequent trial, where Lieutenant Hodgson repeated the story of his sergeant's encounter and told how people in the countryside had pointed out to them the rebels' route. The flight of King before the rebel army marched out to the battle site is no proof of his complicity but suggests rather that he was by this time a disillusioned conspirator who fled on realising that he had been misled by false hopes of a mass rising. And King's employment by the authorities is quite impossible to reconcile with their total unpreparedness for the rising when it came. [s19, *171*; P42; P43]

Bonnymuir and Strathaven were the futile revolts of a tiny minority. The risings were the outcome of radical conspiracy among men who were totally unable to control and direct the events that followed their 'Address'. Underground remnants of the union societies had talked of rebellion during the early months of 1820; their plots were real and not the work of spies or the products of vivid imaginations, though conspiracy was never as serious as fear at times led the authorities to believe. Plotting remained confined to the few; it failed to attract all the radicals, let alone sufficient numbers from the army or the general population to make rebellion a workable proposition. The radicals were insufficiently well prepared to mount a general rising, and the workers were not yet ready to move from striking into revolution.

After the collapse of the strike and the minor risings, suspected men were hunted down, though up to twenty were reported to have fled by boat to London. Sir Walter Scott's future son-in-law, John Gibson Lockhart, commanding arms searches around Airdrie, noted a change in the popular mood from 'savage audacity to fear and sullen submission'. In Ayrshire Colonel Alexander Boswell saw that 'the Radicals are in alarm every where. But I regret I cannot say there is any change in *opinion*. They crouch but are not subdued.' [P22; P5] In fact they were very nearly subdued, for only a few acts of protest remained, such as the storming of an ammunition escort party bound for Glasgow later in the month, and crowd demonstrations on behalf of the condemned men at their execution in Stirling. There were also a few cases of small-scale industrial violence later in the year, but it is impossible to demonstrate any causal link between them and the events of April. [P62; P69]

Following the débâcle of 1820 Scottish radicalism turned away from ideas of revolution and the use of 'physical force' towards the 'moral force' of the 12,000-strong Glasgow Political Union of the 1830s and the strong Chartist organisations of 1838-42. It is not, of course, possible to know the extent to which the lessons of 1820 were responsible for the overwhelmingly peaceful nature of later Scottish radical movements in the hundred years before 'Red Clydeside' re-established its reputation for militancy. Two men who had been imprisoned in April 1820, James Turner, a Glasgow tobacconist, and John Fraser, a Johnstone school-teacher, both played a leading role in upholding the educational and social reform themes of Scottish Chartism and emphasising a gradualist approach to politics. Fraser denounced attempts to turn Chartism towards policies of insurrection, and it is significant that 'physical force' advocates were more prominent in Edinburgh than in Glasgow. Edinburgh had not engaged in rebellion in 1820 and so had no first-hand experience of its futility. [s3, 249-55]

This futility is naturally more evident to posterity than it was to Wilson, Baird and Hardie when they shouldered their muskets and pikes, for they were misled into rebellion by wishful thinking that the people on both sides of the border were either up in arms or prepared to rally to their cause. A harsher verdict was delivered on them by the Paisley radical who recalled that 'every thing was left to a chapter of accidents, and that the leaders, although not spies nor absolutely liars, were never-theless crazy fools, and that by always talking about revolution, they at length imposed upon themselves, and became possessed of one fixed idea, that a revolution would be the result of their nonsensical and mad projects'. [P52; P42] In many respects it was the Pentrich story all over again, and the Bonnymuir rebels' defence counsel, Whig advocate Francis Jeffrey, likened their case to that of Jeremiah Brandreth in 1817. Lord Advocate Rae, prosecuting Strathaven rebel James Wilson, re-marked: 'The case of Brandreth and others, at Derby, is quite similar to the present. . . . It did not diminish the guilt of the prisoner that his expectations were foolish. . . .' [P62]

The year 1820 was the last of post-war 'alarm', and after a decade characterised, though far from dominated, by a few abortive attempts at revolution and rumours of countless others, the period of the 1820s was by contrast one of relative quiet. The so-called 'Enlightened Tories' such as Peel and Huskisson were reversing the repressive approach of the immediate post-war years and reforming policies were implemented which, among other things, repealed the Combination Laws, liberalised the laws of trade, mitigated the savagery of the penal system, and gave political rights to Roman Catholics. This last, coming at the end of a decade of relative political calm and inactivity, was a triumph for the new style of political campaigning and organisation, dependent in part on the alarm that it provoked within government circles, which would seek, with varying degrees of success, to extort concessions from the governments of the 1830s and 1840s by exerting popular pressures upon them.

Within this new political context the threat of revolution acquired a new role. Where previously its advocates had plotted secretly the overthrow of the government, they now openly threatened revolution as a fate that awaited governments which failed to take whatever steps were currently being demanded. Revolution became, if not respectable, at least a conventional threat employed within the tactics of political campaigning and popular protest, and its new role within the life of the nation would pose different kinds of problems for historians from the plots and conspiracies of earlier years. Like many threats it remained most potent when not carried out, and its employment in politics, the art of the possible, was to some extent a matter of elaborate bluff, though some less sophisticated practitioners of revolutionary intent still remained. It is one of the most difficult of exercises to attempt to assess the actual intentions of men whose bluff was never called, and a resort to informed guesswork and speculation on hypothetical situations must be accompanied by no dogmatic pronouncements.

After 1820 it is less meaningful to approach the subject of revolution through a study of popular movements and their actual or potential revolutionary content, the reform movement with its capacity for misinterpretation by its enemies and exploitation by its most militant advocates, and government repression which helped to provoke insurrectionary conspiracies by a refusal to tolerate an open reform movement. After 1820 the individual component parts of the overall picture were to change considerably. Popular movements would proliferate, but be of widely differing kinds: the food-riots would largely disappear, though the farm labourers' riots of 1830 revealed again the possibilities of widespread violent social protest among sections of the population who lacked the political sophistication to communicate their grievances by more socially acceptable means. On the whole, however, popular movements became organised and planned campaigns, usually to exert pressure on the legislature to effect certain changes in the laws of the country. The labourers' riots might have provoked fears of insurrectionary intent, however ill founded, but the political campaigns, which acknowledged parliament as the supreme authority to be petitioned, were hardly full of revolutionary menace. The reform movement too became increasingly difficult to confuse with ideas of revolution, especially as it recovered the patronage of the parliamentary Whigs and became adopted, albeit in diluted form, as the cause of governments. And as governments became more and more accustomed to assuming some initiative on reform questions, even parliamentary reform, they became ever less likely to pursue policies of repression against those who had previously been regarded as disturbers of the peace and fomenters of rebellion. And showing themselves ready to listen to appeals and amenable to peaceful pressure, they were less likely to provoke rebellion through their own intransigence. Only when an impasse had apparently been reached was revolution offered as a tactic of retaliation, and it was offered as a tactic and not as an end in itself.

4 The Reform of Parliament: The Middle-class Threat

Parliamentary reform became a popular movement in the years following the Napoleonic Wars, and it was the hope of many of its leaders that it would become the sole popular movement, for they argued with each discontented group that a reform of parliament would provide them with the means of satisfying their particular needs. Success in 1817 or 1819 would have put their argument to the test, but they were not successful and the needs remained, as they did in most cases after the moderate Reform Bill of 1832. It is not then surprising that a recent study of popular movements in the period 1830–50 should have been concerned with a wide variety of popular agitations of which only two were concerned with parliamentary reform, the campaigns of 1830–2, and Chartism. [s61] The reform campaign retained and increased its status as a mass movement, but its supporters were not consistently active and were always liable to lapse into long periods of apathy and inertia; it was also likely to find itself in competition with other popular movements, such as trade unionism, which offered scope for improvement outside the political sphere, or the Anti-Corn-Law League, which offered a more precise and realisable asset than political rights. Yet at times, particularly during the Reform Bill crisis of 1831–2 and the years of most intensive Chartist activity, the movement for political reform recovered temporarily its capacity to unite large numbers of people behind a common cause and generate a great deal of popular excitement. On these occasions it was unsympathetic rather than repressive government which impeded the reformers' progress, but the result was again to raise the possibility of revolution within British society. This time revolution was being put forward as the ultimate pressure by which coercion would replace persuasion. Its new role as a technique or tactic of protest, rather than as an end in itself, probably meant that its proponents were less enthusiastic about launching their revolution than the zealots of earlier days, but their greater numbers and greater organisation suggest that it could have been greater than, if different from, the kind of threat posed in the post-war period.

The crises associated with the Reform Bill and Chartism certainly pose a different kind of problem for the historian, for here he is dealing not with attempted and failed revolution, but only with the threat of it, and it is more difficult to analyse a threat than an actual attempt. It is also impossible to lay down any objective criteria on what constitutes a revolutionary situation. It might be argued pragmatically that revolutionary situations are empirically what produce revolutions and as there was no revolution there were no revolutionary situations. Against this some would wish to argue that certain situations might well have led to revolutions but for the fact that the necessary steps were taken to avoid this possibility, that revolutionary situations were in being that could have produced revolutions, such as, perhaps, the situation in May 1832 before the passing of the Reform Bill. These situations certainly merit comparison with earlier crises and suggest some conclusions about the possibilities of revolution within nineteenth-century Britain. These terms are to some extent arbitrary and no more than a convenient personal shorthand which has to be explained at some length in the context of the political crises through which they were employed.

In particular, the crises associated with the Reform Act and with Chartism illustrate what men had in mind when they threatened the government of the day with revolution. On both occasions those in power were confronted with threats to their position from others who sought to extort concessions from them. On neither occasion did revolution come about, though this common outcome of the two situations was determined by quite different responses from those in authority, responses in turn determined by the differing relative strength of the parties involved in the two periods.

The crisis over parliamentary reform had two peaks, when revolution is thought to have been a possibility. The first occurred in October 1831, after the House of Lords had defeated the government's reform proposals on the 7th, and riots occurred in different parts of the country which suggested to some that anarchy was near and a possible armed uprising intended. Although some historians have chosen the October crisis as the point at which Britain came close to revolution, closer perhaps than at any other time since 1688, it is fairly generally agreed that the more serious crisis was that of May 1832. Again the Lords refused to pass the government's proposals, and Lord Grey, in despair at the attitude of the peers and the refusal of the King to provide him with the necessary means to coerce them, submitted resignations on behalf of his government. In an effort to save himself from the unpalatable course proposed to him by the Whigs, the King invited Wellington to attempt to form a Tory government, and it was during the days of his unsuccessful efforts, the 'Days of May', that the country was again, in the view of many, close to revolution. And even after the Wellington threat had been removed, the danger did not immediately disappear; a few days of further hesitation prolonged the crisis and kept open the possibility that political change would have to be accomplished by revolutionary means. During this second, a less violent yet more dangerous, period in May, the threat came not from rioters but from the well-organised political unions, from the middle classes of society rather than the working classes whom governments had usually feared in this context.

The political crisis associated with the passing of the Great Reform Bill began in the summer of 1830 against a background of farm labourers' riots in the south-east of England, and industrial unrest, including riot, in many of the manufacturing districts. [s47] Rural and industrial riot was compounded by the election riots which followed the resignation of the Duke of Wellington in November 1830, and which were repeated and extended in May 1831, when Lord Grey persuaded the King to allow him to appeal to the country on the issue of parliamentary reform. During this general election the mayor of Rye witnessed what he described as 'scenes of revolutionary terror', but this disorder was as yet only an extension, as a result of the intensified excitement, of those anarchic displays which so frequently characterised the electoral scene during this period. Not so the riots which were to occur in October. On the 8th of that month the news reached provincial towns that the Lords had thrown out the government's reform proposals, and a riot immediately ensued at Derby, where the jail was attacked and several people killed before order was restored. In nearby Nottingham there were early signs on Saturday the 8th of those assaults on the property of anti-reformers which were to build up so violently on Monday the 10th, when Colwick Hall was pillaged and Nottingham Castle, belonging to the Duke of Newcastle, destroyed by fire. Further violence occurred the following day, including the destruction of Beeston silk mill, before law and order prevailed in Nottingham, and a thrill of horror was felt throughout the country at this first experience of mob violence on a massive scale which arose over the reform issue. Yet even the Nottingham reform riots paled into insignificance in comparison with those at Bristol at the end of the month when, for several days, the town was in the hands of a rioting and pillaging mob which attacked and destroyed a large number of public and private buildings and industrial properties. The death and destruction at Bristol introduced widespread apprehension into political life. There were further riots in the west country at

Tiverton, Yeovil, Blandford and Sherborne, and more were feared at other places after the Bristol troubles, though these fears proved largely unfounded and popular violence essentially at an end. Though the veteran Benbow had welcomed the Bristol riots as evidence no doubt of the popular mood and the power that the people might wield, all moderate reformers rushed to dissociate themselves from these events, fearful of the threat to property that they portended and fearful in the short term of the damage they would do to the reform cause as Tories rushed to portray the disorders as the inescapable consequences of the reform agitation. [s45; s8, *339*]

In fact the moderates probably gained more than they lost from the Reform riots. They were able to exploit the new situation to their advantage, and even riots would eventually be shown to have played no trivial part in the concessions of the Tories and the determination of the Whigs. They had occurred, according to Thomas Attwood, the leader of the Birmingham Political Union, only where the organised power of the unions was weak, and there has been some support among historians for this judgment, which was initially a self-interested declaration. [s4, *253*] Riots were a sign of reformers' weakness, not of their strength, and the antidote was organisation and control; they were also an indication of the inadequacy of existing policing arrangements in provincial England, but this was not a problem open to immediate solution, whereas reform leaders were able to produce almost instant action to strengthen their position. In any case isolated and undirected riots in provincial towns were not a sign that revolution was at hand. On this occasion rioters focused on a national political issue, exemplified locally by the borough-owning Duke of Newcastle in Nottingham or the ultra-Tory Sir Charles Wetherall, recorder of Bristol, but the riots reflected social and economic discontent in the places where they occurred, as they invariably had done in the past, and there was no connecting link between the rioters other than that they were all responding to a common political crisis. Co-ordinated riot in the provinces or extended riot in the capital might have been a different proposition, but the events of October produced only an almost universal desire that they should be suppressed and not repeated. When the crisis of May 1832 occurred, it seemed to Henry Cockburn that the really ominous and fearful aspect of the situation then was the total absence of riot and in its place a calculated determination that could be directed towards the achievement of a mighty purpose. [s8, *403*]

In Nottingham political tension remained high after the riots. There were many rumours in circulation of the arming and drilling of the

Political Union. Lancelot Rolleston, one of the two magistrates who had pursued the Pentrich rebels on 10 June 1817, reported the collection of subscriptions for the purchase of arms, the availability of a musket and bayonet for 16s 8d, and the daily arrival by coach of arms supplies from Birmingham. Undoubtedly some individuals acquired arms and the atmosphere remained tense enough for the town clerk to prepare an escape route for his family through the back garden of a neighbour, but no evidence of systematic preparations was ever forthcoming, and Lord Melbourne was inclined to treat his Nottingham correspondents with a fair measure of scepticism. [P15; P17] This was hardly possible with regard to Attwood's proposal of early November to arm members of the Birmingham Political Union and give them a quasi-military structure and authority for the preservation of law and order. [s61, 45] What was represented as a precaution against further disorders was also seen as a threat to the position of the government, for if Attwood intended no direct military confrontation with the Whigs he certainly intended to stiffen their determination to proceed with reform and show them some of the possible consequences of inactivity. Wellington responded to this new situation by advising the King to suppress the Birmingham Union which was, he said, arming and threatening to develop into a national guard. [s8, 315] The Whigs produced the response intended of them. Grey resolved to press on with the reintroduction of a measure, and Joseph Parkes agreed in secret negotiations on behalf of the Union to cancel the plan in advance of the government's proclamation against political unions. This kind of development illustrates the novelty of the 1831–2 situation. Prior to this time threats and evidence of arming had come from ill-organised working-class groups and had been countered by policies of repression. Now the threat came from a well-organised middle-class group and the government had responded by negotiation and appeasement. A new power was clearly at work within the state.

In fact the Union's position was thoroughly ambiguous, and it is this ambivalence which makes so difficult any assessment of the revolutionary threat of this period. Working-class reformers were quick to suggest that the proposed creation of an armed force was not to guarantee the passage of a reform bill but to ensure that no genuine reform measure would be passed. [P1] Members of the Political Union, wishing to be strong enough to coerce the government themselves, were equally determined that it should not be coerced by the advocates of universal suffrage who threatened more than mild adjustments to the political machinery. These men too were appreciating the need to give themselves teeth. A police spy reported on 21 November that the leaders of the National Union of

Working Classes, meeting at the Rotunda in Blackfriars Road, had instructed their members and supporters to arm themselves immediately; according to Benbow, soldiers would make the best class leaders as they could teach their members how to march and use guns. It is, of course, impossible to estimate how extensive was this process of arming among middle-class and working-class reformers at this time. Attwood later suggested that he had not intended that the unions as such should be armed, but that if individuals chose to exercise their traditional rights as Englishmen that was their business. [s6, 259, 254] Almost certainly many did choose to do so, and it was confidently believed in May 1832 that Birmingham could easily produce an armed force of 1500 men. [P1] A large number of men, from all social classes, must have acquired arms by May, when the air became thick with stories of more intensified preparations for armed rising and of swords and pikeheads that were being manufactured in Sheffield and prepared for use at the barricades following the resignation of Grey on 9 May. [P72] An unofficial armed force far in excess of the regular army could have been collected on behalf of reform by May which, under an agreed leadership from middle- and working-class reformers acting together, would have been capable of causing the government no small embarrassment. Whatever the exact extent of the arming of the civilian population at this time, and this is impossible to calculate, there is good reason to suppose that it was far more extensive than it had been during any previous crisis and that the arms were something more than the sticks and pikes that had created so much alarm in the years after 1815.

On the military side of the proposed rising which was certainly being planned by 12 May, Francis Place remained, according to Graham Wallas, somewhat reticent. [s59, 301] This is hardly surprising in view of the treasonable implications of what he was engaged in at this time. His general assurance that there were plenty of experienced men of military and naval backgrounds ready to organise and conduct military opera-tions is less convincing for the naming of these potential leaders by Joseph Parkes, who had hopes of the Polish Count 'Chopski' and Colonel Napier, of known radical sympathies. The latter, however, later ridiculed the notion that he might have been willing to act in association with a Birmingham attorney and a London tailor against the Duke of Wellington, and the intended leadership certainly supplies a comic opera touch to the proceedings. [s59, 302-3] That is not to say that an armed force could not have been effectively raised and deployed. If armed revolt proved necessary, the Birmingham Political Union was pledged to an uprising and their city was the chosen centre for its beginning. The

Political Council of the Union had been offered by its membership a bodyguard of 1500 men with muskets, and there were enough rank-and-file union members with arms to give Attwood and Parkes an army at their command. [P1] Perhaps it would have stood little chance against an equivalent number of regular soldiers, but the government would never have been capable of putting that number against it even had they been willing to do battle with such a proportion of the civilian population. It has been suggested that this is something they would not have been willing to do, that such a course would have been politically impossible, and that Wellington must have conceded defeat on finding himself in this predicament. [s6, *309*]

Like so many aspects of the planned uprising, this can only be a matter for hypothesis, and the paper army of the reformers is not entirely credible. Armies which are not mobilised never can be, but it is at least easier to believe in the threatened force of 1832 than in the many thousands of 'sworn heroes' who appeared in Luddite threats of 1812 or the pathetic bands of 1817 and the 1820s who were intent on over-throwing the government by force of arms. Armed resistance was to be made if it had to be, yet this was not the central part of Place's plan and remained vague in part because it was expected to become unnecessary. 'Subtler weapons than arms' were to be used against the Duke of Wellington should he become Prime Minister, and men in the City were proud, according to Butler, to think how scientific a revolution might be made in the nineteenth century. [s8, *377*] Even if the House of Commons refused to withhold supply from the government, as it was repeatedly being asked to do, a campaign of civil disobedience could produce the withholding of taxes, and a run on the banks could ensure an even more immediate undermining of the credit of and confidence in any new government. 'To stop the Duke, go for gold' was the slogan coined by Place to inspire the campaign from which Place expected to achieve most success, and if London was not thought to be the natural spot for starting an armed uprising it was certainly the centre of British credit. The advantages of these tactics were that they did not invite military retaliation and that they could be escalated according to the needs of the situation. Almost half of the £3–4 million gold reserve was withdrawn in the crisis, a mere gesture according to Place which simply indicated what was possible, and the beginnings of an impossible situation for a government to face. [P1] According to Cobbett the run on gold was the most effectual of all means used against the King and his potential ministers: all tradespeople in London were refusing to take £5 notes, and some were refusing all banknotes in payment. [P59] On the resignation of

Grey the *Manchester Guardian* had reported a more complete stoppage of business than any public event had previously produced, and it is difficult to believe that the accession of Wellington would not have been met with a complete breakdown of the economic life of the nation, with large numbers out of work, and the government unable to cope with the sheer bulk of disorder that would have arisen. [s8, *383*]

Again, it is possible to see in these manœuvres not only a sophistication of technique beyond anything previously envisaged by tavern conspirators or workshop insurgents but a real power actually being exercised, which was strong enough, if pushed far enough, to accomplish that which earlier plans could never have the remotest chance of achieving.

If these economic sanctions were insufficient the provinces were to be mobilised, though the intended function of the excited crowds in the Midlands and the North was not as marchers upon the capital in traditional rebel style. The delegates who had gathered in London following Grey's resignation on the 9th were to return home if Wellington's appointment were announced, and were to be replaced in London by deputies who would form something like a Committee of Public Safety. The leaders back in their towns would take command and prepare to act, with Birmingham the first place where the barricades would go up. It was estimated that 7000 troops, the bulk of the army, would be kept occupied in London by demonstrations and other threats to the safety of the capital, and the uprising would be free to establish itself first in the Midlands and later in other centres if the government did not succumb to this pressure. Place claimed to be in communication with influential men in all the large towns and to have organised lists of all sympathisers who could act in providing local leadership. Addresses and proclamations were all prepared, and in less than five days, Place reported to Hobhouse, Grey's Minister for War, the soldiers would all be with the insurgents. There would be no serious fighting and no more than a few days' commotion. [p1]

Thus were the plans prepared and a revolutionary strategy worked out quite different from anything previously imagined by furtive conspirators who had contemplated assassination or a midnight rebellion as the means to power. This was an open conspiracy: it could be so because of the virtual non-existence of any government during the middle of May: it had to be so because the whole point of the scheme was that the enemy should be deterred from doing something in the knowledge of what consequences would follow from his action. The plan was for revolution, however respectable its organisers, however determined they were that a revolutionary seizure of power should not precipitate social revolution in Great Britain. If the middle-class reformers were influenced by the Bristol riots to 'call it a day' and settle for a very limited reform measure, they were certainly not prepared to 'call it a day' over the lengths to which they were prepared to go to ensure that this limited measure should become law. [s47] Or so, at least, they said. And whatever defects in the revolutionary plan were glossed over by Place, whatever doubts remain about his capacity and determination to lead a revolution, his was a more carefully prepared plan, a more widely supported and probably effective plan, than any of its predecessors. However near Britain came to having a revolution in 1832, the crisis did produce a better scheme for accomplishing revolution than anything previously devised.

In the event the reformers were successful without needing to implement their plans. Wellington abandoned his commission to form a government on 14 May, Grey returned, and by 19 May was assured of all the necessary behaviour from the Lords and the King to ensure the passage of the Reform Bill. The Pentrich and Bonnymuir rebels engaged in overt rebellion, and their efforts can be examined as historical events. The parliamentary reformers did not, and their efforts became essentially of academic interest as the prelude to a non-event. Yet the interest of these efforts is considerable, for they produced what was arguably the plan of revolution most likely to succeed in nineteenth-century Britain, and they placed the country in what was arguably a revolutionary situation.

It is easier to recognise the merits of the blueprint for revolution in 1832 than to calculate the nearness of revolution in that year. Within this general area the probable role of the working classes is only one of a whole series of imponderables. Traditional views of the industrial north of England, drilling and preparing for social war, of industrially aggrieved and therefore politically conscious workmen willing to rise up against the Lords for denying them parliamentary reform, of reform eventually carried 'chiefly by working class agitation' and under the threat of revolution in which the workers would have played the main part, all these almost certainly exaggerate the interest felt by working men in the reform campaign, and their capacity for organisation and action on behalf of this cause, especially when their energies were being simultaneously absorbed by the agitation for factory reform and by trade union activity in general. [s58, 237; s12, 65]

By the end of 1831 Place's Political Union had twice the membership of its working-class rival, the National Union of Working Classes, though as early as 7 November it had been claimed that there were 104 towns with 'low unions' and that these supplied the Rotunda with better provincial links than Place possessed at this stage. On the one hand Place admitted that the National Union of Working Classes had a better hold on working men than his own union, especially in the great manufacturing cities, for the notion of class co-operation had made little headway outside Birmingham; on the other he felt able to make scornful remarks about the unrealistic assumptions of the working-class leaders that their followers were ready to rise *en masse* and take over their own affairs; if a rising were announced, only a tiny proportion would ever hear about it, and without middle-class assistance they would never accomplish any national movement. [P1] As it was, their relationship with the political unions was one of mutual hostility, and while the latter grew stronger they themselves continued to suffer from all those weaknesses of popular apathy and divided leadership which characterised working-class movements of these years.

Although the Days of May witnessed alarming strikes in the mines of the North-East, there was no working-class organisation in being to mobilise and direct working men throughout the country towards a common purpose. The organisation which Place and Parkes directed appears to have regarded the workers as potential demonstrators who might tie down the army in London, or potential unemployed who might choke the poor law administration or otherwise embarrass the government and make its work impossible. In all cases the workers were a passive bloc to be manipulated to serve Place's purpose rather than an initiating group with a positive and constructive contribution to make. And this remained true in spite of the rapprochement that was finally achieved in the final stages of the crisis, when leaders of the Rotunda acted in co-operation with Place and moderates united with extremists in the provincial towns too. They still disagreed about the merits of the Whig reform proposals, but they showed a common determination to have nothing of Wellington, and the Days of May marked the high point in their co-operation. A revolution might have been used by the extremists to their advantage, as Wallas argued, and so they had no need to hesitate in co-operating for once with Place's schemes. [s59, *299*] Place for his part remained steadfastly determined not to further their aspirations and to make use of them only so far as it served his purpose to do so.

It is the implicit fear of working-class extremism that supplies the enigmatic quality to this middle-class plan of revolution, places so many question marks beside the names of men like Place and Attwood as potential revolutionaries, and prompts the view that revolution in this situation was never a probability. Place's much-quoted aphorism, that the National Union of Working Classes wanted reform to promote revolution while his own supporters wanted it to prevent revolution, has raised grave doubts about the lengths to which he was prepared to go, and therefore the ultimate weakness of his position, which was based on a series of fears. The Bristol riots had shown the red light to all parties, it is argued, and the reform leaders feared to attempt harder bargains 'with the support of the streets'. [s47] But Place also feared that if a new Bill were not quickly introduced after October 1831 Whigs, Tories and middle classes alike would find themselves with social revolution upon their hands. He was thus plagued by conflicting desires to have the affair settled, but to avoid pushing too hard in case an undesirable conflict arose, and this remained the essence of the calculated gamble that he was required to take. If the governing classes acted foolishly they would provoke resistance, and power might end up in the wrong hands, for revolution, according to the *Poor Man's Guardian*, could only be effected by the poor and despised millions and was therefore the greatest object of alarm for the middle-class reformers; it might lead, as Place realised, to popularly elected government, for which the people were not ready, and was therefore undesirable both for the present mischief and future trouble that it would cause. [s57, *890*; P1] Yet the arrival of Wellington in power, according to Francis Jeffrey, might lead to a rampant soldiery in use against the populace, retaliation, the massacre of anti-reformers and the destruction of their property in all the manufacturing districts, a situation of veritable anarchy, while his eventual defeat might lead to the destruction of all government in state and church, which was equally to be avoided. [s8, *410*]

The prospects were fearful in every direction and a nice calculation was required over the greater and lesser evils. Were the middle-class reformers more afraid of the working classes than they were annoyed at the behaviour of the Tories and the Whigs, more afraid of initiating a revolution which they could hope to control than of the consequences of the eventual terror into which the politicians would lead them if allowed to go unchecked, a terror which they could not hope to control? Of course, the middle classes feared social revolution, which made them reluctant to dabble in political revolution, but Place and his fellow leaders evidently judged that this was more likely to follow from inactivity than from activity on their part. The risks involved in promoting revolution were carefully assessed and evidently considered insufficiently inhibiting to deter them; the risks involved in the alternative were impossible to assess and too frightful to contemplate seriously. And so Place became a reluctant but apparently determined advocate of revolutionary action.

The efficacy of extra-parliamentary pressure, as well as its resolution, has been called into question by the seeming intransigence displayed by the politicians, Whig and Tory, their apparent immunity to public pressure, and their indifference to the debates and developments that were taking place around them. These factors have prompted observations that the whole crisis was both precipitated and resolved within parliamentary circles alone and, by implication, the conclusion that the threat of revolution was irrelevant to the solution of the problem and that a revolutionary situation could have been effective only if a revolution had been precipitated. For all the public meetings, the demonstrations and the petitions, it is argued, what stopped Wellington from forming a government was not public opinion but the refusal of Peel to serve with him and his consequent inability to construct a ministry acceptable to Parliament. Similarly, what put a stop to the opposition of the Lords was not the Birmingham meeting of 7 May, which had been called to do this, but the threat to create new peers. The Whigs came back into power not, as the reformers chose to believe, on the shoulders of the people, but as a result of Westminster manipulations which made their return the only possible solution to the problem; by May, it has been said, the agitation had moved significantly from the streets, and the success of the Bill would be resolved by the manœuvres of parties and not by the intervention of the lower classes in the towns. [s61, 45–6]

There is, of course, a truth in all these claims, but they are none the less misleading. It is true that the run on the banks never fully materialised and that Place's plan for a national uprising was stillborn, but this was only because these projects had already achieved their purpose by being threatened and did not require to be put into action. It is also true that the political unions were best organised for insurrection three to four days after Wellington's accession to power had ceased to be a practical issue, but the King, the Lords and the Whigs still needed to be coerced before the drama was over, and for that purpose the external pressure remained vital. Wellington himself might have seemed indifferent to the public mood, might even have been so, but the riots of the previous October had been a warning of what social anarchy could entail, and the vast repeated demonstrations of public indignation and determination had left the Whigs in no doubt that reform could not be shelved or passed by the hand of Wellington. The successful mobilisation of public opinion by the political unions in April and May convinced the

Whigs of the need to proceed and convinced the political unions that they had the power to make them do so. Cobbett's words to the government on 19 May were no more than a pardonable exaggeration: 'The people put you to power, the people have kept you there, and if you again attempt to set them at defiance you will become nothing, and nothing you ought to become.' [P59] Whig retention of power was now conditional upon a willingness to use it in a particular way. In this situation it could hardly be maintained that the parliamentarians had not been successfully subjected to the external pressures of public opinion.

But the greatest doubt that remains about Place and his plans concerns the possibility that the whole scheme was just a gigantic bluff. One leading exponent of the 'bluff' interpretation emphasises that the middle-class reformers were conducting a calculated propaganda campaign in which they sought to give the impression that revolution was the alternative to reform and used organised pressure as an instrument of intimidation, which is correct. [s30, 77–85] It is also probably true that the leaders were prone to doubts as to the strength of their following, which was natural enough, and that the conflict had generated a surprisingly small amount of class antagonism and little open hostility to the great national institutions, though it was maintained that the King's behaviour had made more republicans than the writings of Tom Paine. [s8, 415] But these last two factors, though interesting, are hardly relevant to the kind of limited action that Place had in mind, and would have encouraged him to proceed rather than inhibited him. The later claim of J. A. Roebuck in 1848, that public opinion had been described not as it was but as it was meant to appear, was self-praise for alleged ingenuity and a tactical withdrawal from a position that was proving so embarrassing to the middle classes when they self-righteously criticised the threats made against them by the Chartists. [s30, 77–85] During the ten days of greatest crisis, from Grey's resignation of 9 May to his return with full powers to pass reform, there is ample contemporary testimony to the belief that revolution was a very serious possibility. Attwood in Birmingham on the 10th declared his determination to take up arms if it should prove necessary, while deputies in London on the 12th confirmed the willingness of the people to rise *en masse* and accepted that resistance must be made if Wellington formed a government. As late as the 18th, four days after Wellington's failure, the unions were even better organised to insist on their demands for full power to Grey: 'we are otherwise on the eve of the barricades'. Place two days later expressed the opinion that the country had been within a moment of general rebellion which, Joseph Parkes confirmed, he and his friends would have led whatever the risks. [P1] With the organisation at their command they had confidence in their ability to avoid these, and to the end gave no sign that they were not prepared to act. Revolution would have meant failure for their policy of coercing the government by threats, but it seemed a lesser evil than a rampant Wellington.

The test never came, which must have been almost as much of a relief to those who would have been required to fight revolution as to those who would have had to conduct it. The urban riots of 1831 had exposed the totally inadequate policing arrangements in the towns outside London, and some effort would be made to rectify these by the Municipal Corporations Act of 1835, though another round of disturbances, by Chartists in 1838-9, was necessary before action was taken to establish a rural police. In the absence of a police force it always fell to the army's lot to preserve law and order in the first half of the nineteenth century, and in the last resort it was the army which stood between Britain and revolution. This force of about 11,000 might serve well enough in particular areas on particular local issues; it could not, however, police a whole country when a national issue threatened trouble in many areas. When the London leaders attempted in April 1832 to calculate the number of men who could be used against them, they estimated that there were 7000 soldiers in the London area for the defence of the capital, and this number, according to Place's reckoning, could be kept fully occupied by demonstrations and other threats to public order. This would leave a mere 4000 to cover the rest of the country; as *The Times* had remarked on 1 November 1831, the regular troops were not sufficient in an emergency. [P1] Even the few riots of October had put them under severe strain. Few troops could be spared to take care of Bristol when other places posed little threat, and that town had experienced days of anarchy before order was restored. The authorities, later faced with riots in smaller towns, were afraid to leave Gloucester unguarded lest that too should succumb. [s8, *310*] And this was simply a situation of unplanned spasmodic rioting, not to be compared with the threat that organised insurrection could pose.

The other problem concerning the army, in addition to its size, was its loyalty. This again was never put to the test and so judgment cannot be much more than speculation, but there are some slight indications that the army was not entirely reliable. Joseph Hume's declaration that the soldiers would not fight was perhaps firmly within the traditional belief of earlier figures on the verge of revolution that the army would defect: this belief was backed, but hardly substantiated, by the rumour that soldiers had promised to fire high. Members of the Hertfordshire Yeomanry had resigned on the fall of the Whigs, and on 14 May it was reported that the soldiers stationed in Birmingham were threatening to join the Political Union. Alexander Somerville testified that the Scots Greys would do their duty in suppressing riot or attacks on property but would not act against public meetings or attempts to march with petitions from Birmingham to London. It has very reasonably been questioned whether 150 troopers tinged with disaffection could have succeeded in coercing Birmingham, and it seems unlikely in the situation of May 1832 that they could have relied on the supplementary assistance of the yeomanry at such a time in such a place. [P56; s6, *301, 307*] But even with perfect loyalty and solidarity in the army's ranks, it would clearly have been powerless, in view of its numbers, to contend with the kind of uprising that Place had the means to launch by 12 May. His prediction that all soldiers would have come over within a few days might not have been fulfilled, but they would at least have been powerless to go on fighting beyond that time. [P1] Prior to 1832 there had been, apart from isolated examples involving individual soldiers, no difficulty in using the army against rioters and rebels from the working classes. It seems probable that refusals to obey orders would have been more numerous in 1832 than ever before and that the military forces would have found themselves impossibly outnumbered.

And so the moderate parliamentary reformers had their way, and the precedent they had established by extorting concessions under threat of armed resistance was to be an acute embarrassment to them when the Chartists began to demand further measures of parliamentary reform and to employ similar tactics for their achievement.

5   Chartism: The Working-class Threat

Chartism was the greatest of the popular movements of the first half of the nineteenth century in that it embodied, when at its height, the hopes and aspirations of perhaps millions of people spread over the whole country, whose different social and economic grievances from a huge variety of local contexts were temporarily merged in a massive protest movement that aimed to turn Britain into a political democracy. However middle class the background of some of its leaders, Chartism was a movement of the people's own; its mass support was working class, and its programme was first to enfranchise the working classes and then, hopefully, to tackle those social and economic discontents that had prompted people to try to change the nature of political representation. Chartism had two characteristics that neither reformers nor revolutionaries of the 1790s had ever been able to bring together in one movement, political consciousness and popular support, but the popular support was never mobilised for anything more revolutionary than the points of the Charter, and a right to share in the running of the parliamentary system was sought only within the workings of that system and not by attempting to overturn it.

Yet it is clear enough that Chartism presented the governments of the 1830s and 1840s with a succession of crises, during which it was widely believed that attempts would be made to achieve revolution by force. The first of these occurred in the autumn of 1839, after the break-up of the Chartist Convention. In early November a body of armed men marched upon Newport, Monmouthshire, amid rumours of co-ordinated rebellion in different parts of the country, rumours which persisted into January 1840, along with some evidence that they might be fulfilled. The second was in August 1842, when the Chartists attempted to exploit industrial unrest for political purposes, and serious disturbances combined with extensive strikes to threaten the survival of the government. The last was in the spring and summer of 1848, the year of European revolution, when the government faced a Chartist demonstration in London which might possibly have been turned into an uprising and was later troubled by a number of conspiracies to overthrow the government by force.

The revolutionary threat posed by the Chartists is as difficult to elucidate as that of the parliamentary reformers, for the historian is still dealing with hypothetical situations and what might have been, as well as seeking to clarify and interpret the events that did occur. Two things make this latter task particularly hard; one is the sheer impossibility of discovering all that needs to be known, about the rebellious conspiracies for instance, before judgment can confidently be passed, and this has led more and more people to accept the impossibility of conclusive verdicts; the other is the inescapable ambiguity of practically everything that the Chartists ever said or did. Whether they were threatening force, arming, or even holding a public meeting, their activities were open to a variety of interpretations which has not narrowed down with the passing of time. Nothing is quite what it seems. And this arises because the Chartists themselves were never sure what any particular activity might lead to, whether a meeting might produce a riot, or a riot a revolutionary uprising. So much of their conduct was so speculative and its outcome so unpredictable, that it is impossible to ascribe precise intent at particular moments of time. And because the threatened clash never materialised between the forces of government and the people in arms, it has been possible for individuals to go on believing in whatever prescribed outcome suits their personal inclination. Such matters as the full extent of popular support for an armed uprising or the probable loyalty of the soldiery in such an event are by their nature insoluble problems.

The Chartists certainly talked more openly and more often about their readiness to revolt and use physical force than any previous campaigners, and a distinction has traditionally been drawn between the advocates of physical as opposed to moral force. William Lovett provided what he no doubt believed to be a defence of the moral force position when he quoted Sharman Crawford's opinion that 'when the application of physical force is held forth as the moving power for attaining the reform of our institutions the aggregation of the moral power which can alone render physical force either justifiable or effective is destroyed'; but this is an ambiguous statement and certainly does not rule out the possibility of using physical force in some situations. [P47] Lovett himself conceded that government aggression might produce legitimate resistance and was arrested for putting his name to a document from the Birmingham Convention which justified popular resistance. Some leaders rejected the antithesis as entirely false: Sketchley of Leicester denied its implication that physical force could not possess a moral basis, while Ernest Jones believed that physical force must always remain as a legitimate last resort of self-defence. [s3, *134*; s49, *22*] In the words of a Carmarthen resolution of April 1839, oppression would justify resistance, and what was right warranted all expedients necessary to achieve it. [s66, *142*] Even the most correct advocates of non-violent means of persuasion upheld the traditional right of individuals to possess arms; many who opposed the actual use of force none the less upheld the right to use it; while many of the orators would conclude an inflammatory speech with an injunction to keep the peace, which they believed allowed them to be counted still among the advocates of peaceful means. [s3, *133–4*] The divisions are not then clear, and there were many positions between the physical force extremists and those whose excursions into popular protest went no further than public petitioning. Though the advocates of outright physical rebellion were few in number, so too were those who totally excluded from their plans any intention of pressuring the government by at least a display of the physical power that the Chartists were capable of mounting.

The ambiguities were conveniently ignored when the leaders were blaming each other for the movement's failures. Lovett later described the rapid progress made by Chartism, among middle as well as working classes, until the violent talk of the extremists scared away possible friends and gave the government the excuse it required to pursue repressive policies. [P47] This view assumed that the only prospect of success lay in the working classes' ability to demonstrate their worthiness to be enfranchised and the willingness of the middle classes to co-operate with them; a peaceful movement would prove the one and ensure the other, as a result of which parliament would be persuaded to grant their request. This was almost certainly an unrealistic assessment of the situation. A more accurate appraisal was made by the physical force advocates, who saw that their reforms would not come by concession at this time and would have to be taken by force if they were to be achieved at all. They were right to see this as a question of power, not gentle persuasion, and wrong only in their belief that they possessed enough power to get their way. In 1832 a power struggle had been resolved peacefully because Place and his colleagues had commanded a force of such strength that the enemy had chosen not to fight. The Chartist leaders doubtless hoped for similar success by impressing upon the government that they were too formidable a force to be denied and resisted. And so they must, according to O'Brien, petition with one hand and hold a blunderbuss in the other, a style of petitioning that never failed, and they must hope that the blunderbuss would never need to be fired. [s20, *42*]

This war of nerves was fought by a violence of oratory that was never matched by violence of conduct. O'Connor's injunction to 'go flesh every sword to the hilt', his praise for the one torch that was worth a thousand speeches, and his appeal for martyrs; Vincent's call to every hill and valley to be ready to send forth its army; Harney's alternatives of suffrage or death; Stephens's question as to when they should commence burning and destroying the mills; and Benbow's requirement that every boy of twelve should possess a stiletto to run through the guts of anyone who offered opposition – all these were rhetorical devices to frighten the government and were not intended to be taken literally. [s66, *101, 133, 140*; s3, *27, 46*] This was the language and the tactic of bluff, to extort concession by inducing fear, to make the imagery so frightening that the reality was never put to the test. The authorities were to be so impressed by the talk that action would be unnecessary; this was the hope of most, and coercion by threat of force was the limit of the means they were prepared to employ. A few were also prepared to employ the force if its threatened use should prove an insufficient pressure.

In this context the arming of the Chartists must be seen as a political device as well as a preparation for military conflict. Britons of all social classes had a traditional right to possess arms; if they demonstrated their social equality, they would move a step nearer to political equality by showing what a formidable force the working classes constituted. And if the demonstration of power was insufficient, the ultimate tactic was the employment of this newly constituted force. The Chartists of Leicester were urged by John Markham to do as the gentlefolk and ornament their mantelpieces with arms, but how long they would continue as ornaments is difficult to say. [s3, *105*]

It was almost a characteristic mark of nineteenth-century political crises that members of the working classes would acquire arms, and this happened in 1839, 1842 and 1848, but as with Luddism and the reform crisis of 1831–2, this did not necessarily betoken an intention of engaging in armed rebellion, though it did make working men a more fearsome prospect and a greater force to be reckoned with. 'Arm, arm, arm', was the repeated injunction of Chartist leaders to their followers, and there is no doubt that the open display of arms and the discharge of guns at Chartist meetings helped to produce panic among magistrates and the propertied classes. Through the autumn and winter of 1838–9, rumours circulated and some evidence began to build up that weapons were being acquired by the working classes in different parts of the country; in

Newcastle where the ironworkers were said to be manufacturing small cannon, grenades and pikes; in Yorkshire and Lancashire, where men were held up as an example to the rest by Bronterre O'Brien in March 1839, for the way in which they had equipped themselves; in South Wales where muskets were being ordered from Birmingham, pikes being manufactured, and weapons sold and distributed among supporters; even in Wiltshire where the Trowbridge blacksmith had received orders to manufacture pikeheads, and magistrates were in no doubt that local Chartists were armed. [s20, *81*; s66, *132, 138, 143, 154*; p14]

Just how extensive this arming was cannot be said, nor can it be known to what extent armed Chartists could have been converted into fighting men had the need for this arisen. Rumours of drilling invariably accompanied the other tales in circulation, though even these activities were no proof of intention to fight. Samuel Bamford had trained his parliamentary reformers to march in orderly processions prior to Peterloo, and John Frost organised his Monmouthshire Chartists in military formation with the alleged intention of producing an impressive demonstration of their strength at the Monmouth election, though they ended up by demonstrating their military weakness as a fighting force. [s66, *187–8*] Renewed arming and drilling was reported during the subsequent crises of 1842 and 1848, but no Chartist army again appeared in the streets, and it is questionable whether any but a few committed revolutionaries seriously intended that it should. It was a long step from possessing weapons to joining in revolution, as had been previously demonstrated on countless occasions. Julian Harney, thinking to turn general strike into revolution, believed that arming was an essential precondition of striking, but for most who participated in the exercise it was an assertion of right, an aggressive urge being fulfilled, and a campaign being mounted to terrorise the government and its supporters into concession. [s47, *70*] However well it satisfied the personal urges of individuals, it failed in its political purpose and demonstrated the need to keep the workers under control rather than the necessity to do business with them.

Most of the Chartist energies went into demonstrations rather than planning insurrection, and it was unfortunate for the success of the cause that the great convention of 1839, the most spectacular of them all, should have been a demonstration of Chartist weakness rather than strength. Here again there is ambiguity present. The Convention was to sit during the period when the first petition was presented to parliament, the size of its electorate and the nature of its members demonstrating the unrepresentative nature of the House of Commons and the moral authority of the Convention to speak for the working classes. It was ineffective in this capacity but it had another role. It had the appearance, even the intended appearance, to supporters and opponents alike, of being almost a rival to parliament itself, an anti-parliament set up in opposition to the legally constituted body and thereby a subversive organisation. In one view the very existence of the Convention created, in the minds of millions, an alternative to the existing state, and some of its members were ready enough to endow it with some degree of legislative authority. [s20, *61*; s64, *105*] But it failed totally to impose any unity or authority on the working classes, let alone on the nation as a whole, and the pompous pretensions of some of its members did not require to be taken too seriously by the other House of Commons at Westminster.

As a talking-shop and a large-scale demonstration, it probably served a similar function to that of the public meetings, as a safety valve for energies that might otherwise have gone into rioting. The large meetings, especially the torchlight meetings in the North in the winter of 1839, were a very satisfying experience for those involved, because they provided the excitement and stimulus of involvement in action against the government without the risks attached to actual conflict, the dressings and emotions of insurrection but a safe bed at the end of the meeting. [s33, *29*; s15, *105*] The appearance of large crowds of people, many of them armed and some of them discharging their guns to prove it, gave Chartism a menacing aspect to those whom it was intended to menace, and even a peaceful demonstration hardly deserved the name when it implied a threat and indicated the kind of physical strength that could be mobilised. Nor was there any guarantee that peaceful demonstrations would not turn into something else, that South Wales miners meeting in May would not take an *ad hoc* decision to rescue Henry Vincent from gaol, or that the simultaneous Whitsuntide meetings of 1839 would not be the signal for the start of street fighting and the beginning of insurrection, for barricades were actually erected at Stone in Staffordshire. [s26, *151*] After all, simultaneous mass meetings had been the policy of the extremists in the autumn of 1819; they were at least a means of assembling large numbers of people and could have been a first step towards involving the masses in revolutionary action.

John Frost's march upon Newport, probably intended as a great demonstration of strength with the majority of participants unclear of their purpose, ended unexpectedly in bloodshed and being classified as a treasonable rebellion, a clear example of how demonstration might lead to revolution and how unpredictable was the course of events. Similarly, the grand demonstration that was to accompany the presentation of the third petition in April 1848 was anticipated by some Chartists as being a possible means by which power could be achieved, and was certainly guarded against by the government as if armed insurrection were the purpose of the meeting on Kennington Common. On 10 April there were also armed bodies of miners and factory workers converging on Manchester from neighbouring towns who would have been confronted by cannon in the streets of Manchester had they arrived there. [s26, *271*] To categorise this as a march, a meeting, a demonstration, a riot or even a rebellion is not easy, for it would be mistaken to regard these as clearly defined and separate techniques of protest which could be rationally selected and carefully carried out.

Rioting in particular was impossible to predict and control, both in its outbreak and in its consequences. Historians have noted at this time the declining role of riots and uncontrolled violence in popular agitation and seen this as evidence of a growing political consciousness among the working classes, but contemporaries could hardly afford this comforting observation or even be in a position to make it. [s33, *29*] For nearly a week in the middle of July 1839 Birmingham experienced incendiary riots, during which trade was halted and many fled the town; nor was this the traditional hungry mob intent to loot shops, but a politically inspired and angered populace provoked by the actions of the local authorities. [s50, *77*] There had earlier been riots in Llanidloes during which the Chartists had controlled the town for some five days. [s66, *157*] During the 'Plug Plot' strikes of August 1842 there were again violent clashes with the army in the West Riding and north Staffordshire, where magistrates' homes were attacked and burnt, while 1848 brought riots in England and Scotland before the April crisis and further riots in Yorkshire afterwards, during which, according to Gammage, Bradford was for a day in the hands of the Chartists. [P39] Uncontrolled violence of the kind produced by rioters usually contained the least political menace to the government and was a conventional law and order problem rather than a political problem of its own survival, but though the riots that did occur were in fact contained and did not lead on to other things, their danger was, in the political situation of the time, that a town temporarily under Chartist control might become the inspiration and base for further assaults and that simultaneous riot, under some kind of leadership or control, might turn into the insurrection that many feared; for, not having experienced revolution, contemporaries were not qualified to predict in what form it might appear and how it might be initiated.

If riots were an unlikely, though by no means impossible, route to political power, the same cannot be said of the weapon of the general strike, which seems in retrospect the best hope the Chartists had of realising their ambitions. [s25, *75*] Once more the enigmatic quality is present, for the general strike, perhaps more than any other technique of industrial or political protest, is of imponderable proportions. In the years 1838–42, when its purpose would have been avowedly political, it could have become the instrument of revolution and much more than a means of coercing the government over a limited objective. This is indeed how it was viewed by Julian Harney, who believed that arming came before striking, as a general strike must provoke a general conflict for which the workers should be adequately prepared; O'Connor in the *Northern Star* similarly opposed the 'Sacred Month' of August 1839 on the grounds that the workers were not universally armed, and the decision of the Convention to revoke its strike decision probably resulted from a realisation that this could mean revolution, which they were not prepared to initiate. [s50, *84*] A more limited action was envisaged by Lovett, a partial strike to test the feelings of the country, a demonstration, hopefully, of Chartist potential rather than an attempt at direct coercion to bring down the government. [p47]

In fact neither the comprehensive nor the limited approach was attempted, but a confused endeavour which demonstrated only the inability of the Chartists to rally mass support and utilise the weapon of industrial action. The 1839 attempt to graft industrial action on to political protest was reversed in 1842 by the attempt to graft political action on to industrial protest during the so-called 'Plug Plot' of August, when Chartist leaders tried to utilise for their own purposes the industrial troubles of the North and Midlands by asking workers to remain out on strike until the Charter had been granted. This was a stroke of political opportunism, in spite of the Home Secretary's belief in a joint conspiracy of trade unionists and Chartists to bring down the government. [s3, *389*] Thomas Cooper was later to present a well-balanced account of the conflicting arguments that surrounded this unexpected opportunity for Chartist exploitation in August 1842. For his part, he believed the time had come when the fighting must start; if the strikes could be spread, the government would be threatened with paralysis, and would attempt to quell the strikers; a general outbreak must necessarily follow, and a united people would triumph in a trial of physical force. His opponents listed the weaknesses of his case: that the workers were unarmed and unprepared; that they were ill-clothed and underfed, which was why they were striking; that a few days of sleeping in the fields would kill them even without the artillery of the regular army. In spite of these persuasive arguments, McDouall produced his dramatic appeal to the 'God of Battles', and the Manchester Convention of 17 August voted in favour of a universal strike for the securing of the Charter. [P36]

The defects of the decision were soon very evident. This was a strike from a position of weakness not strength; the workers had no resources and were much more vulnerable than their employers, who were themselves being accused of precipitating the strike for their own purposes; they joined in many cases only under compulsion; their efforts could be sustained for only a few days; and their political motivation remained minimal. The special constables and militia, it has been said, were far more ready for violence than the leaderless bands of unemployed workers who briefly roamed the countryside, and the strike, far from achieving the Charter, only alienated trade unionists from the Chartists, who were wrongly blamed for the whole wretched business and its unsuccessful outcome. [s61, 122] What had been in theory perhaps the most likely way of coercing, or even overthrowing, the government had turned into another demonstration of Chartist ineffectiveness. The use of industrial action for political purposes demanded a much more carefully prepared plan than the Chartists ever produced, and was dependent on a much more politically conscious and united working class than the Chartists were ever able to call upon for support.

The only other hope for the Chartists lay in armed insurrection, an implicit admission that they had failed in their attempts to coerce the government by threats and must seek therefore to replace it by force. Many leaders spoke the language of insurrection, but even committed revolutionaries like Harney were men of rhetorical speeches rather than action. The actual plotters tended to be men of second rank, while the leaders, with few exceptions, steered clear. [s33, 29] Feargus O'Connor, for instance, frequently promised his support and his leadership, but promises were all he gave, and when the authorities opened his correspondence from May 1839 they found no evidence of his involvement in any revolutionary plots. [s43, 86] The Chartist Convention of 1839 had neither the inclination nor the ability to organise armed insurrection, despite its frustrations in all other fields, and if the 1848 Convention later seemed to be engaged in a trial of strength with the government, this, it has been argued, was not of its own making but arose through the determined mobilisation of the government and middle classes against the Chartists. [s50, 166]

In the absence of leadership and co-ordination from the top, the conspiracies were hatched at the local level, though invariably with the belief that it was possible for simultaneous risings to be accomplished, a belief dependent for its fulfilment on a degree of organisation, planning and popular support for rebellion that never existed. In the December and January of the 1839-40 winter, following the Newport rising of November, rumours were again rife that rebellion was being planned to release Frost or somehow avenge the fate of the men of South Wales. The date of 12 January was evidently fixed for the rising, and O'Connor's ambiguous response to approaches had created some belief that he was to lead the movement. The signals for the rising were given from Dewsbury, but they met with virtually no response beyond an attack upon the police at Sheffield and a pathetic show of force at Bradford later in the month. [s62, *136-7*] The plotting was temporarily at an end and the authorities made their customary punitive descent. It was renewed in the summer of 1848 after O'Connor's failure at Kennington Common, when 'foolish schemes of impracticable rebellion' were devised to try to give Britain her share in the '48 revolutions. [s26, *294*] Government action against the open agitators had created a conspiratorial underground movement, a not unfamiliar pattern, and attempts were again made through the summer to co-ordinate action in the different districts through the activities of the much tried but never successful system of delegate links. Thomas Cooper visited London in 1848 and later recorded that plotters and planners were as plentiful as blackberries in that year. Like Bamford in 1817, Cooper was visited by men who told him of their plans for revolution, which he declared himself unwilling to listen to; the Chartists seemed wilder to him in his maturity of 1848 than he and his colleagues had been in their own days of turbulence, but they were no more capable of staging a successful revolutionary coup than their predecessors had been. [p36] Their plans were penetrated by spies and *provocateurs* in almost traditional style, and the new contribution of the Irish Confederates acting in association with the northern extremists brought no accession of strength to the revolutionary cause. Both 12 June and 15 August were dates fixed for simultaneous risings, but internal dissension and external activity of espionage and arrests ensured the failure of the conspirators and the conviction of further men found guilty of levying war against the monarch. [s43, *137-8*]

The feeble nature and failure of these later conspiracies forces into greater prominence the events of November 1839, when bodies of men gathered in a few Monmouthshire towns for a march upon Newport, the taking of which was widely supposed to be the signal for further risings in the Midlands, the North, and the North-East. There now seems to be little prospect that the events of October and early November will be accurately and adequately reconstructed, and regional historians, whether of Manchester, Leeds or South Wales itself, have found it impossible to know how far their own particular local leaders were involved in an overall plan of which the march upon Newport was a part. Separation of the truth from the rumours is not possible in this 'obscure corner' of Chartist history, and reasonable inferences are the most that can be drawn from the information available. [s3, 79]

It seems reasonable, for instance, to believe in the existence of some form of notion that risings were to occur in all the principal Chartist centres, such as Birmingham, Bradford and Newcastle, that groups in these places had been in communication with each other, and that they awaited some form of sign, possibly an initial rising from the Welsh, to set them all into motion. Hetherington in London heard reports on 29 October of possible risings that were to take place in Wales and the north of England, and Frost, the Newport leader, was in contact with other areas, yet there is no reason to suppose that there was a commonly agreed plan that a co-ordinated rising was to occur at a prearranged time, only a general understanding or feeling that something was to be attempted. The secret and therefore obscure exchanges that took place between the various districts, when plans, however vague, must have been discussed, contrast with John Frost's openly published instructions to his supporters in the *Western Vindicator* to organise themselves and form tithings in each parish, which can be interpreted as a plan for a revolutionary army curiously made public or as a plan to demonstrate local Chartist strength by a massive and organised turnout at the Monmouth election, which was Frost's declared intention. The failures of the Chartist Convention, the rejection of the petition, and the collapse of the Sacred Month must certainly have frustrated the militants of South Wales and left them with physical force as the only untried policy, but whether their intention was simply to demonstrate their physical strength or actually to use it cannot with certainty be said.

The more that has been uncovered about the Newport Rising, the more difficult it has become to ascribe precise motivation to those responsible. The charge against the marchers placed the severest interpretation upon their conduct, that they were levying war against the Queen by marching in battle array, seizing arms, firing upon the magistrates and the army, attempting to capture Newport, and seeking to change the laws of the land by the use of force. Yet apart from marching and exchanging a few shots, the accused had done little to make their intentions clear, and one interpretation of these events has been that the whole affair resulted from the officer commanding soldiers in the neighbourhood of the Westgate Hotel losing his head at the sight of an apparently armed mob. This seems a very generous and mild view of the importance of the incident, yet the prosecution were not able to prove their theory of a general insurrection and had to withdraw it, and it is easier to destroy possible motives behind the march than to say what its precise purpose was. The defence showed conclusively that there was no question of sending signals of victory by stopping the mail. The entry into Newport made no sense as a possible assault for the taking of the town, and the release of Henry Vincent from Monmouth jail could not have been achieved by an attack upon Newport. The events of 3/4 November bear so little resemblance to the wild rumour that had previously gone round the country about impending rebellion – for general insurrection there was none – that it has been not unreasonably suggested that the march was not part of any long premeditated plan but was decided on only a few days in advance and that its organisers and participants had nothing more certain in mind than a resolution to make an effective demonstration of their strength. In this they failed, and at the same time acquired notoriety for staging Chartism's most prominent attempt at armed insurrection. It is perhaps indicative of the weakness of the insurrectionary strand that its best known representatives acquired their reputation by accident rather than by design. [s66]

The failure of the Chartists to mount a successful revolution has led to inevitable speculation of a somewhat mischievous nature about the kind of revolutionary strategy and tactics that should have been followed. The entertaining but futile exercise of prescribing an alternative course for history to have taken assumes some shred of justification only if it throws light on the actual events of the past and is not simply concerned with what might have been. The imposition of a rigid theoretical framework upon the events of 1838–48 is not particularly helpful if it leads only to suggestions that a one-class revolution was predestined to failure and that victory could have come only through 'the fruitful co-operation of two or more exploited classes'. [s44, *250*] The prevailing situation is the one that requires explanation, not an imaginary one of two or more exploited classes acting in fruitful co-operation, whatever that might mean, and in that situation it is relevant to observe that simultaneous risings could not be successful as long as the leaders of local followings acted without the necessary unity and decision. [s50, *83*] But this is true of all aspects of Chartism, and it naturally follows that if Chartism was weak in all its aspects it was weak in any particular one of them.

The problem of staging a revolutionary movement, apart from the general weakness of the Chartists, arose in part because, as Asa Briggs points out, only a small minority had given any thought to this problem and these few had been ineffective in their thinking. [s3, *302*] In particular, little thought had been given to the problem of conducting a revolution in an industrial, increasingly urban society, and thoughts of revolution through general strikes had gone little beyond the belief that something would happen if the working classes could be brought out on strike and the government confronted with such a hostile and vital section of the population. In so far as people had made a study of revolution it was the French pattern that they knew rather than a British pattern which they sought to devise. Harney, for instance, the most intelligent and best informed of the revolutionaries, thought in terms of street-fighting and barricades, of *sans-culottes* rather than industrial workers in factories and mines, of a revolutionary *putsch* rather than a mobilisation of the working classes. [s20, *108-9*] This is not to say that his approach had no chance of success or that the alternative approach would have brought victory. All that can safely be said is that what was attempted did not bring victory and that little thought appears to have been given to what methods of waging revolution were most appropriate to the conditions prevailing in Britain at this time.

The outcome of the trial of strength between the government and the Chartists was empirically a victory for the government. The strengths of the government and the weaknesses of the Chartists were together greater than the weaknesses of the government and the strengths of the Chartists, but the practical outcome of this contest has not prevented speculation about the degree to which government resources were stretched in coping with the problem. The basic weakness of the government's position was revealed in Greville's remark that it was impossible not to feel alarmed when the vast amount of population was compared with the repressive power in the possession of the government; yet defence requires only the mobilisation of enough strength at the right time in the right place, and this the government was able to accomplish. [s62, *213*] With the professional police only just beginning to spread outside London, the principal, indeed the only reliable, peacekeeping force within the country was the regular army, and when General Napier was appointed to the Northern Command in April 1839 he had only between five and six thousand soldiers at his disposal, a meagre number with which to keep the North and Midlands in a peaceful condition and make plans to cope with a population that might threaten rebellion at any time. He needed to husband his resources very carefully under the deluge of appeals to his Nottingham headquarters that were made by alarmist and cowardly magistrates who each assumed his own district the centre of greatest danger. The North was deficient in barrack accommodation, which Napier tried to make a condition for supplying an area with troops, and the persistent substitute of billeting made his soldiers vulnerable to both attack and corruption. It was an article of faith, almost certainly misplaced, among intending rebels that the soldiers were sympathetic with the insurgents' cause and would not fire against them if required to do so, and Chartist leaders assumed that a large proportion of men in the ranks were themselves Chartists. In fact Napier had far less trouble from his own soldiers than he had from an incompetent magistracy, which was a theme of his many communications to the Home Secretary. Inertia, cowardice and obstruction all bedevilled his relations with the civil body. [P14; s26, *139–41*; s32, *33–4, 164–70*]

Yet for all these weaknesses the government never seems to have doubted the ability of the army to cope with anything that the Chartists were capable of throwing at them, and little evidence was ever forthcoming to support the view of sympathy or disaffection in the ranks that would assist the rebels. When Frost and his men found themselves face to face with regular soldiers in the centre of Newport, they realised that their former expectations were totally unfounded. Alexander Somerville, the radical ex-soldier, warned the Chartists that they would be powerless to resist the artillery of professionally trained soldiers if street warfare were begun, and Napier himself was at great pains to point out to them the certain consequences of a contest against the army. [s64, *132*; s62, *128*]

The other bulwark of the government's position was the increasing willingness and enthusiasm of middle-class people to step forward and enlist as special constables on the side of law and order. This was progressively more noticeable as Chartism advanced, for there had developed by 1848, in one view, a more militant middle-class consciousness in London than the workers had yet achieved, and the middle-class response to the April crisis was to demonstrate their own strength rather than that of the Chartists. [s3, *299*] After all, the formidable 150,000 or more special constables enlisted to contend with O'Connor's followers almost certainly outnumbered them many times over and were a remarkable assertion of what has been called the 'silent majority', who were shown not to favour the Chartist programme. [s62, *204*] Together with 4000 police, 8000 regular soldiers, and the 1500 Chelsea Pensioners whom the revitalised Duke of Wellington had at his command, these volunteers constituted a comforting display of strength to those who had suspected that the country was vulnerable to Chartist attack. [s50, *165*] Outside London too there was effective rallying to the side of authority, as at Loughborough, where 500 specials joined the yeomanry, the dragoons and the police in an effective display of force which included the prevention of a meeting which O'Connor had planned to hold in the town. [P66; S3, *117-18*] The government always had enough strength to cope comfortably, and middle-class willingness to become involved grew as Chartism developed, though police growth remained uneven and responded only to moments of greatest emergency.

Although neither government nor army leaders were as worried by the threat of general insurrection as the panic-stricken magistrates who communicated with them, Napier appears to have given a lot of thought to the strategy to be employed against the Chartists, in particular to the prevention of a possible co-ordinated march upon the capital from the provinces. He took great pains to explain to the Chartists the impossible task that would confront them if they attempted to put an unofficial army in the field against his regulars, who would not allow them to march ten miles without attacking them with cannons and muskets and who would not permit their survival for three days. [s62, *128*; s3, *380*] Napier has been almost universally praised for his restraint and moderation, as well as for his skill, but his moderation would not have overcome his determination had his hand been forced. Nor was the government reluctant to use the full force of the law when that was thought necessary. In May 1839 a royal proclamation was issued against drilling and local authorities were given the discretion to arm special constables and loyalist groups and to arrest Chartists in possession of arms. In the winter of 1839-40, when fears of revolution were at their height, hardly a Chartist leader escaped imprisonment, according to Graham Wallas, and the troubles of August 1842 were met by a further purge of Chartist leaders after the Home Secretary, Sir James Graham, had decided that force alone could subdue this rebellious spirit and dispatched troops to Manchester, the West Riding and the Potteries to take vigorous action against the strikers and rioters. [s59, *375*; s3, *388*; P14] And, again, in 1848 preparations were so thorough and the government response so determined that O'Brien told the crowds, in a realistic assessment of the situation on 9 April, that the government was too strong for them. He was unfavourably received by his audience, but his judgment was no less accurate for that. [s50, *165*] When the rejection of the third petition was followed by a period of plots, those that warranted action were quickly uncovered and destroyed.

The other factor in the internal balance of power was the strength of the Chartists themselves, and this is particularly difficult to calculate because no one effectively mobilised it. Some people have persisted in the belief that Chartism was a movement of massive inherent strength and potential which was badly let down by the failures of its leaders to take advantage of the opportunities that presented themselves. The strength of the Chartists is to some extent a matter of faith and belief, instanced by the assertions that by 1838–9 the 'gathering masses were ready and burning to fight for the right to eat and live'; that they possessed a great urge to fight; that they would have responded if only their delegates and leaders had shown the necessary faith in them and led them into action; that in the industrial areas of Lancashire, Yorkshire and South Wales, only military force could prevent a rising among a population of such determined unanimity: but a limited military force did prevent a rising in spite of the supposed unanimity of such large numbers of people. [s20, *57, 84, 89*; s59, *375*]

There are, in fact, many indications of the weakness of Chartism's popular support, which the zealous leaders and the frightened middle-classes quite misjudged in their hopes and their fears. Harney, planning an armed demonstration in London on 6 May 1839, did not manage to organise one and showed how lacking in militancy was the area close to the seat of government. [s50, *66–7*] The Frost rising, whatever its intent, was widely condemned among Chartists and confirmed their apathy or even hostility towards the idea of revolution. The December/January plots in the West Riding met with a negligible response and showed the impossibility of mobilising large numbers there in support of such action. When masses of people were engaged in active protest, during the Plug Plot of August 1842, Harney conceded that the majority of the trade unionists were not Chartists, and few would be inclined to argue that those involved were displaying any political consciousness. [s20, *138*] The lessons of 1848 were again that desperate conspiracy had no popular backing and that apathy was as important as disorganisation in preventing more effective political action.

This is not to deny that problems of organisation were important in preventing the Chartists from mobilising the support which they did possess. It has been rightly argued that a working-class movement must act through the institutions and organisations created for its own purposes. [s20, *106*] By 1838 these were still non-existent or singularly defective, throwing the movement back upon the whims and fancies of individual leaders and the *ad hoc* organisations of secret committees and travelling delegates, who contributed more confusion than illumination to the matter in hand. Napier believed the Chartists not too dangerous because they lacked the necessary organisation, they had no good leaders, and could not resist making money even from supplying each other with arms. [s64, *129*] When revolution was intended, the problem of communication proved insuperable, as the confusion surrounding Frost and Newport demonstrates. A popular uprising cannot be openly planned because it is illegal, but if it is secretly planned it can never be popular. This had been the dilemma of the revolutionaries in the 1790s, and it remained unresolved in the 1840s. The problems of rallying the masses in simultaneous action over a wide area were no more satisfactorily tackled by the Chartist conspirators than they had been by the Pentrich or Bonnymuir rebels, and the mid-century efforts illustrated exactly the same weaknesses that had fatally affected earlier enterprises: no clear idea of purpose, lack of organisation and discipline, total misjudgment of popular support beyond, and even within, the particular area, mistaken notions about the willingness of the army to fight, susceptibility to bad weather, all these were as damaging to Chartist rebels as they had been to their predecessors.

Whatever the long-term importance of Chartism for the development of democracy or a working-class consciousness, it was a failure as a short-term political exercise because it was easily brushed aside and did not achieve what it set out to do, and its failure is particularly stark when contrasted with the success of the middle-class reform campaign of 1831/2, which employed the same kind of tactic of threatening the government with dire consequences, even the use of force and revolution, if its demands were not conceded. Successful political blackmail had been carried out in 1832, and this second attempt was no more immoral than the first, only less likely to succeed. It ill became the middle-class victors of 1832 to lecture the Chartists on the illegality of the methods that they were proposing to employ, for the same sauce was now being prepared to serve the proverbial gander. The difference between the two situations was almost entirely in the resources at the command of the two petitioning parties. Such were the apparent resources at the disposal of the middle-class reformers that the government never dared to call their bluff. The middle classes were so strong that they had to be accommodated. The working classes were so weak that they could be disregarded. They were invited to go ahead and do their worst, which they did. Their bluff was called and bluff it turned out to be, because the working classes could not summon forth the revolution that their leaders had threatened. Among the proposed 'ultimate measures' that the 1839 Convention approved was the request to people that they should be willing to withdraw their money from the banks and prepare themselves with the arms of freemen to defend the laws and constitutional privileges of their ancestors. [P47] They were dealing in myths, for they had no constitutional privileges and no money.

6 Prospects of Revolutionary Success 1789–1848

When people seek, as they do seek for whatever reason, the period when Britain came nearest in modern times to experiencing revolution, they usually look at the years between the outbreak of the French Revolution in 1789 and the more widespread, though less important, uprisings that characterised the European scene in 1848. These limits do seem meaningful for Britain as well as continental Europe. At the one end political activity in Britain was much intensified as a result of the French Revolution, which inspired much adoration and some attempts at emulation: at the other end the '48 revolutions abroad had parallel movements at home, and with their failure decades of intermittent depression and disturbance gave way to an era of domestic calm. This then is the period when the revolution would have happened if it was going to happen, for, according to E. J. Hobsbawm, there was no time since the seventeenth century when the common people had been 'so persistently, profoundly, and often desperately dissatisfied' as they were between the closing years of the French Wars and the mid-1840s, no times when large masses of the people had been so revolutionary as they were during these years. [s25, 55]

Within this period particular years have been singled out as the most 'likely' moments for a successful revolution. 1812, for instance, has had its claims advanced by F. O. Darvall, who emphasised the difficulties of the government in its confrontation with the Luddites; the distresses of war, the involvement of the army overseas, the absence of a police force, and the widespread nature of disturbance in the spring of that year. [s16, ch.15] After this time, he believed, it would become increasingly difficult to mount a revolutionary assault upon the government, though it has been argued here that the situation in May 1832 was particularly dangerous for the government and could have led to armed resistance on a broad front.

Whether this would have produced a revolution depends on how the term is to be defined and how successful the middle-class leadership would have been in controlling the events they seemed prepared to set in motion. A successful middle-class attempt to coerce the government, albeit by the use of force, in order to make an adjustment to the political system would not, for some, be sufficient to justify the title of revolution. They would look rather to the use of the power achieved than to the manner of its seizure, and for them a much more fundamental restructuring of the political system and society as a whole would be the criterion by which revolutionary action would need to be measured. Clearly this was far from the intention of Attwood and Place in 1832, and it was not people of their kind whom contemporaries had in mind when they reiterated their fears of a revolution in the late eighteenth and early nineteenth centuries. The revolution was to come from the working classes, and it was their threat which seemed to menace the established order.

The causes of revolutions or revolutionary situations cannot be stated with precision or general agreement. Causal links of any sort are difficult for the historian to establish with certainty, but the general problem of determining what causes what appears in acute form over the explanation of revolutionary situations. Ever since de Tocqueville made his simple yet profound observations that the French Revolution occurred in a country that was not the most reactionary in Europe, after a period of attempted reforms, among a peasantry that was not the most backward and repressed in Europe, and at a time when that peasantry was considerably better off than at earlier periods, there has been a compulsion to ask whether revolutions are not born of rising expectations rather than depression and despair. For example, it might be argued that the Peasants' Revolt of 1381 occurred because commutation of labour services was so far advanced that the remaining ones seemed intolerably onerous. Similarly, it might be tempting to interpret the political discontent of the first half of the nineteenth century as a reflection of growing economic prosperity arising from industrialisation, which stimulated demands for both greater prosperity and political advance, demands created by rising expectations. This would be a difficult thesis to substantiate. When Rostow constructed his celebrated social tension chart on the arbitrary assumptions that bread prices and the buoyancy of the economy were together the most likely indicators of social unrest, he produced a graph that demonstrated pictorially, with fair accuracy, the years of greatest political crisis. Hobsbawm felt that his assumed link between economic misery and social movements could be taken for granted, and most historians of this period have, indeed, accepted the reasonableness of this position. [s24, *130*] They have found their political crises in periods of economic distress and political apathy in periods of economic prosperity. Chartism has been particularly susceptible to this kind of interpretation, and in the earlier period the rise and fall of political excitement in Lancashire, 1816–20, has been similarly explained. [s42, *98, 105, 154*] For the century as a whole the contrast between the mid-Victorian period of prosperity and political indifference and the earlier decades of coinciding economic and political crisis is very striking.

In terms, too, of the participating people, there has been a general tendency to find the political activists among the distressed rather than the prosperous, though there is not necessarily a positive correlation between degrees of distress and degrees of activism. If the outworkers, the weavers, stockingers, croppers, woolcombers, nailers and other representatives of domestic crafts that were offering their employees deteriorating standards long before their numbers declined, were not uniformly imbued with revolutionary consciousness, they were at least among the most politically active groups within the working classes and contrast strongly with the factory workers, who turned to politics only to pursue a sectional interest, such as factory reform, or at times of acute economic depression, such as 1842. Perhaps the weavers or the stockingers most involved were not the most depressed of their kind, for they had evidently the time to look beyond the problem of bare survival, but they were certainly representative of depressed and declining trades. Their inspiration must have been memories of the past rather than expectations for the future, for the plight of their trades had given them little on which to build expectations. Conversely, the skilled trades and their skilled, therefore better paid, members contributed little to political radicalism in the nineteenth century, and were shaken out of their complacent sectionalism only at the end of the century by, among other developments, a threat from the law that needed to be countered by political retaliation on a broad front. [s24, *278, 289*] There is not as yet a sufficiently detailed and comprehensive analysis of the people concerned in the extremist political movements of the first half of the nineteenth century to permit firm conclusions about their economic background and its influence on their political activities. Yet it seems unlikely that such an analysis would support the view that revolutionary politics derived from rising expectations of wealth and accompanying political status and recognition rather than from deprivation and distress. Only the middle-class threat of May 1832 offers any support to this thesis, and this was quite exceptional as a revolutionary threat in these years and contrasts with the working-class threats in almost every way.

The two revolutionary crises of 1817 and 1820 occurred against a background of economic distress. The Duke of Newcastle and H. G. Bennet, M.P., men poles apart politically, interpreted the 1817 troubles in the same way. The former looked to returning prosperity to restore tranquillity and make the lower orders more cheerful and contented; the latter, too, saw discontent as the outcome of distress. [p63; p13] The Lords' Committee of Secrecy in June argued that distress in the manufacturing areas had 'exposed the labouring classes to perversion and disaffection'; a year later it welcomed the increased employment that would bring peace to the labouring classes. [p63]

Both rebel and army leaders accepted the existence of local economic distress as an important factor in the build-up of a revolutionary situation in the weeks that preceded the outbreak. From Nottingham Major-General Lyon gloomily reported on 13 May that stocking-making, the principal trade of the area, was in a poor state and had little prospect of revival, while General Byng reported from his headquarters at Pontefract on 25 May that the local population would become really composed only with the advent of better times; with bread and meat currently so high-priced and labour so cheap stability was not likely. [p16] Similarly, on the rebel side, Thomas Bacon, the Pentrich leader, was alleged to have expressed a wish for either plenty of work for the population or nothing at all; with the former people would be happy, with the latter they would be so desperately unhappy that they would be willing to act to put things to right. At a later stage, when Bacon was trying to shift responsibility for the abortive rebellion, he was still arguing that only the existence of public distress had permitted the government spy Oliver to excite the disturbance in the East Midlands. [p14] It was said in December 1816 that the labouring poor of Nottingham and district were experiencing worse conditions than for forty years. A poor harvest had doubled the price of bread over a few months and put potatoes beyond the reach of the poor, a situation that continued throughout the spring of 1817. [p67]

The jump from social distress to political action was one which the champions of the rebels were quick to infer from the course of events as they unfolded in May and June 1817. The distresses of the poor, said defending counsel Thomas Denman, had driven them to a state of desperation; men had been hungry and miserable and in consequence 'to a certain degree discontented', he explained with mild touch. Lawyer Cross, in defending Jeremiah Brandreth, the leader of the Pentrich rebellion, drew a similar inference; a season of scarcity combined with a want of employment had together destroyed the high expectations raised by the return of peace: the prospects of increased trade and growing prosperity had been shattered and vast numbers of honest and industrious workers had been driven to the verges of famine; the rebels had fought for bread, 'a bigger loaf and altered times'. [P44]

Such an interpretation – a plausible and conventional explanation of why men are driven to political extremism – was in fact challenged by the prosecution, who found little in the condition of the rebels, their speeches or their conduct to suggest that their primary grievances were economic. It was difficult for the defence to maintain that the Pentrich rebellion was virtually a bread march when the rebels had quite clearly demanded not food but arms and manpower from those whom they visited on their route, and it must be conceded that the defence was not able to demonstrate a direct causal link between distress and rebellion. It would none the less be folly to suppose that because the rebels did not formulate a precise list of economic grievances and a precise set of proposals for their removal they were not to some extent motivated by their economic discontent. The vain talk of plum pudding and a hundred pounds for each man, though hardly a realistic and practical aim, is still some indication of the longings and yearnings that men experienced and the conditions that gave rise to them. [P14]

The Scottish rebels of 1820 had displayed a far greater concern for political rights than their English counterparts and no inclination for physical self-indulgence; yet here too there was a general understanding that better times would result from political emancipation. With Britain in the grip of cyclical depression in the winter of 1819–20, Andrew Hardie's trade of cotton-weaving and his native city of Glasgow were in a sorry state. The cotton handloom-weavers were the most severely afflicted under the unregulated influx of Irish and Highland migrants and demobilised soldiers into the trade, and the general economic depression added the workless of other trades to the already swollen surplus of workers who would prefer to work at any price rather than starve. Ayrshire weavers, by the summer of 1819, were working a 96-hour week for five shillings, from which trade deductions such as loom rent and candles still had to be made. From Canada a migrant complained that in 1819–20 in Glasgow he 'had to labour sixteen or eighteen hours a day, and could only earn about six or seven shillings a week . . . in a damp shop'. Such working hours led Scotland's Lord Advocate to complain in the House of Commons that the Sabbath was being profaned by weaving. [P22; P45; P69] The less fortunate had no such opportunity for profanity, for towards the end of 1819 half of the estimated 32,000 handlooms in Glasgow and neighbouring areas were

5   MTH

totally unemployed. Lord Provost Monteith reported that 'the very depressed state of our trade . . . has thrown out of employment altogether an immense number of labourers, but chiefly weavers, while those who have employment have it at such low rates that their wages are not at all adequate to the support of themselves and their families'. Even 'large families, who are employed, or partly employed, cannot jointly earn the price of scanty food for their daily wants, leaving nothing for clothing, education, furniture, rent, and other necessities'. [P22; P69; P45] Everything, including clothes and bedclothes, was offered for pawn. On 9 December 1819 H. G. Bennet informed the House of Commons that 'In the neighbourhood of Glasgow the people had been forced to carry their furniture and clothes by degrees to the pawnbrokers, and . . . the pawnbrokers, having advanced their whole capital on these pledges, were nearly in the same distress'. [P63] Parish relief, private charity and emigration aid together were grossly inadequate to meet the needs of the situation, and by late 1819 there was an acute local awareness that funds and time were running out. In a vain bid to rescue the worsening relief situation the Glasgow Committee for the Relief of the Industrious Poor began renewed fund-raising on 1 January 1820, but the fears of Lord Provost Monteith, voiced the previous August, were about to be realised. 'As long as the funds raised by subscription last, I entertain the strongest hope that the peace of the city will be supported, but if they are exhausted before we have a revival of trade I dread the consequences.' In the first week of April the consequences were upon him, a general strike, the Strathaven rising, and the Bonnymuir Rebellion. [P69; P45; P22]

Over the whole period 1789-1848 the years of political crisis were invariably periods of economic crisis too. The price of bread had traditionally been the best ready guide to the probable disposition of the people, but the development of industry and the dramatic growth of overseas trade added the new elements of cyclical depression and technological unemployment to the economic discontent that would prompt men towards political action as well as congregating them in a way that made their political menace seem all the greater. But economic discontent is probably the condition of most of the people most of the time, yet they are not permanently on the brink of revolution. Nor are revolutions usually inspired, organised and led by the most economically depressed within a society. Political awareness is a more necessary attribute than poverty for the revolutionary leader, and political grievance is just as much an ingredient of the revolutionary situation as economic depression. And if the Industrial Revolution introduced new factors into the causes of popular discontent, no less did the French Revolution, in some part because of the economic consequences of the Revolutionary and Napoleonic Wars, in large measure because of its effects on popular politics and men's ideas of the rights which they possessed as human beings. Traditional notions of freedom and popular rights associated with a mythical golden age in Saxon times before the imposition of Norman rule, the idea of justifiable resistance to tyrannical governments, upheld by Hampden in his refusal of Ship Money, defended by all those who took up arms against Charles I, and reinforced by the political classes as a whole in the expulsion of James II in 1688 – all these were brought up to date and givern modern expression by the successful American revolt against the governments of George III and more especially by the overthrow of the *ancien régime* in France. The right to resist oppression, according to Cobbett in 1815, always exists; it was referred to by the Scottish radicals in 1820 and repeatedly by the Chartists in their long contest with the forces of authority. [P59]

Apart from providing an outstanding example of accomplished revolution which others might wish to copy, the French Revolution gave rise to an enormous political debate, in which working men featured for almost the first time. Though excluded from parliament as well as from government, the working classes could not henceforward be excluded from the arguments and discussions that surrounded these subjects, however desperately successive governments might endeavour to enforce their exclusion. Such bodies as the London Corresponding Society, with its 'membership unlimited', demonstrated the growing political awareness created by the French Revolution and initiated the demand for an extension of political rights, which was the ideological content of the reform and revolutionary movements of the next half-century.

But not only did governments deny the political rights; they also denied the means by which they might be achieved. However serious-minded and earnest the artisans of the London Corresponding Society, however law-abiding their intentions and peaceful their methods of persuasion, their demand for democratic rights was a revolutionary demand, and it remained so even throughout the period of the Chartists. Equality of political rights could well be a step towards social equality and had to be resisted in however respectable a form it manifested itself. Whenever it was advocated it provoked fears, genuine or pretended, that reform must end up in revolution if allowed to go forward, and to advocate peaceful reform was at times almost as great an offence as to plot rebellion. In the 1790s the government feared public reform meetings as a threat to law and order and as one step away from a revolutionary mob; petitioning might be their avowed aim but armed insurrection, it was feared, was their ulterior purpose. Reform campaigns were suppressed, and in their place appeared the very revolutionary conspiracies which the government had previously feared. Again in 1816 the Hampden Clubs, like the Corresponding Societies earlier, provided connecting links between districts and a possible organisation by which revolution might be plotted and accomplished. They were suppressed, through the suspension of habeas corpus, and in their place appeared the underground conspirators.

In the period 1790–1820 governments behaved predictably and perversely, through fear of the possible as much as hostility to the actual, by repressive legislation and other intimidation of reformers, depriving a minority, but by 1816 a fast-growing minority, of people of legal outlets for their grievances, and leaving plots and conspiracies as the sole remaining protest technique open to them. The revolutionary underground, whenever it appeared throughout those years, seems to have been almost the determined creation of stubborn, short-sighted governments that failed totally to appreciate that the surest means of avoiding revolution was to keep protest open and within the limits of the law. By the time of the Chartists the lesson had been learnt and the revolutionary conspiracies were a negligible part of a lawful reform movement which by now involved millions of people and had to endure all the frustrations of repeated denial of its wishes. Before then they seemed to follow, as if by prescription, every principal measure of repression and coercion adopted by the government, and on two occasions, 1817 and 1820, gave rise to actual insurrections which took revolution out of the realm of theory and hypothesis and into that of practical politics.

The abortive revolutions of 1817 and 1820, however feeble they were as movements against the established government, do at least provide some basis for judgment of the strength of the revolutionary threat in these years, and the most abiding impression left by them is their similarity to each other in the weaknesses that they both illustrated. Each was a purely working-class movement with no middle-class involvement, both had high, but totally unrealistic, notions of the strength that they possessed and the support they would receive, and in each case the numbers prepared to participate in armed rebellion were pathetically small; both embodied vague ideas that successful rebellion would somehow lead to economic improvement, but neither laid down how this was to occur. They had also similar notions of revolutionary strategy in terms of the mobilisation of the local countryside and the taking of the big town of the area prior to joining up with similar movements elsewhere.

The principal thing that the rebellions had in common was their hopelessly weak organisation and the total inability of the intending revolutionaries to mount and carry out any scheme which had the remotest chance of success. Villagers who openly discussed their plans in a Pentrich public house a day before their intended rising in the presence of two newly appointed special constables or others who allowed a Hussar to ride off with a copy of a treasonable address which they had presented to him, these were not men of sufficient political grasp and experience to lead successful revolution in early nineteenth-century Britain. Such men, it was always believed, the Burdetts or the Cobbetts, were ready to take command when the initial blows had been struck, but the initial blows were always struck so feebly that the national figures were spared the embarrassment of having to decline to participate. In their absence, the plotters enjoyed the illusion of possessing great strength, and this they derived very largely from the few personal links that were established with other parts of the country, the so-called delegates, who might, like Thomas Bacon of Pentrich, be actually delegated by a meeting in Nottingham to attend another in Manchester or Sheffield, or Oliver the Spy, a self-appointed delegate who worked for the government; or almost unknown men such as Sellers of Manchester, who visited Scotland early in 1820; John Porter of Paisley, who visited England in February of that year; or William Smith of Carlisle, who was appointed to the rebel committee in Glasgow on 22 February. Such men could do no more than speak for themselves or the small handful of men who knew of their existence. They were not organisational links but superficial contacts, not demonstrations of strength but almost certain sources of weakness and causes of folly, for they were rarely able to look beyond their own personal intrigues and enjoyment of assumed power to the real world on which they were supposedly reporting.

Organisation meant knowing what people would do to support them in other parts of the country. Both sets of rebels thought that they would be receiving support elsewhere and both were mistaken. Organisation meant being prepared for the rebellion when it came, yet there was no evidence for this in either case. If the rebels themselves were incapable of putting an armed force on to the streets, and this proved to be the case, it meant ensuring the support of the soldiery, and this was often talked about. In Scotland abortive attempts were made at approaches and it was known that there would be no help forthcoming from the army; in England nothing was done, and so it remained the vain, yet confident, hope that the soldiers would act with the rebels when the time came. But soldiers under oath had much less reason than the civilian population at large to be willing to join in armed insurrection, and there is no evidence in either England or Scotland, in 1817 or 1820, that the rebels could count on the willingness of any but a tiny minority even of the latter to join them in taking arms against the government.

The difficulty has repeatedly been stressed of converting secret conspiracy into mass revolt, of exploiting widespread economic distress for the purpose of widespread rebellion, and this has been seen in part as a technical problem of keeping rebel plans away from government eyes and at the same time making them known to a sufficient number of people for rebellion to be effective. But there was more to the problem than technicalities, for the population as a whole was apparently not only difficult to inform but difficult to persuade as well. A strike might involve many thousands and handbills might disseminate information among large numbers of strikers, as Scotland proved, but this was a different matter from persuading large numbers to participate in armed insurrection. Not only were the rebellions of 1817 and 1820 not well-organised movements; they were not popular movements either.

It can, of course, be argued that the weaknesses of the revolutionary movements of 1817 and 1820 do not necessarily prove the weakness of the revolutionary movement throughout the period 1789-1848, and the temptation has not been resisted to argue that both movements went off at half-cock because of government infiltration and did not adequately represent the strength of the movement which produced them. [s57, 733-4; s19, 133-45] Even if this view were to be accepted, and it is a piece of nonsense where Scotland is concerned, the ability of the government to influence rebel movements so decisively would only be further evidence of their inherent weakness. Far from being typical of the situation as a whole, the abortive rebellions do indicate the general weaknesses of revolutionary movements throughout the period and do give a fair indication of why successful revolution was never accomplished in these years.

In the half century that preceded the National Charter Association, the nearest approaches to a national popular organisation were made by such bodies as the Corresponding Societies, the Hampden Clubs, and the National Union of Working Classes, and all these aimed at parliamentary reform, not revolution. The rebel organisations were small *ad hoc* affairs of secret committees and travelling delegates, too weak to threaten authority, too vulnerable to betrayal and exposure to make membership of them a safe pursuit. The bigger the area that they attempted to cover the larger the network they tried to establish and the more vulnerable they became, to the infiltration of spies, difficulties of communication, misunderstandings and problems of all kinds. The technically most successful working-class rebel organisation of the period was probably that of the Nottinghamshire Luddites, a local affair, the most spy-free and the least political of all such enterprises; but where attempts were made to organise a rebel political movement on a national scale, the sheer administrative task of initiating and co-ordinating such an undertaking proved an impossibility. The conspiracies never became national movements, and the Chartist conspirators experienced all the frustrations, misunderstandings and delusions that had tormented their predecessors. Nor did the plotters ever manage to find the right balance between secrecy and publicity which their schemes demanded, and the summer scene of 1848, again one of underground conspirators hatching fiendish plots known only to a few, including representatives of authority, suggested that not much had changed over half a century and not much progress had been made in the business of planning revolutions.

Nor was there much change in the extent of popular support for armed rebellion over that period in spite of growing political consciousness among the working classes. If it was true of the 1790s that the revolutionaries were too few in number to be dangerous, too localised, lacking in national leaders, and lacking above all a link between themselves and the masses, the same was almost equally true of 1848. Henry Cockburn believed that the lower orders of the 1790s seemed to take no particular interest in anything, which was hardly accurate in that matters of personal survival would usually prompt popular action. Yet a food-riot betokened only the most primitive political response, and inertia and apathy would continue to work for a long time in favour of established institutions and against those who sought to mount a popular challenge to them, even when greater educational opportunities had made such a challenge more feasible. The government interpreted popular involvement in post-1815 reform movements as a portent of incipient mass revolt, but this prediction remained totally unfulfilled. The popular movements never became revolutionary and the revolutionary movements never became popular. They remained instead the work of a tiny minority of conspirators who tried in vain to rouse the mass of the population from the apathy or antagonism that were evidently felt towards the solution which they advocated.

In view of such evidence of weakness on the revolutionary side, the explanation of the non-occurrence of revolution in the late eighteenth or early nineteenth century does not require to be sought in the strength of the government's position and the forces at its command. It is true that the government possessed an army that was loyal and that the attempts of the United Scotsmen and the United Irish to persuade troops to defect met with no success, even if the fleet mutinies of 1797 did cause some unease and seem to threaten the possibility of leaving the country open to foreign invasion. It is true that the army was for many years the only organised force that could have resisted revolution had a showdown come, despite the multitudes of spies and the growing numbers of police forces who contributed their small part to the preservation of law and order in the first half of the nineteenth century. The army coped very well in difficult years such as 1817, 1819, 1820 and during the various Chartist crises. It had a harder time contending with Luddism in 1812, a movement of some grass-roots strength and organisation if no political ambition, and in 1832, had the middle-class reformers decided to implement their plans, it is difficult to see how it could have prevented them. Government in modern Britain, even the Britain of the unreformed electoral system, has been government by consent, and the relative size and strength of the governed on the one hand and the coercive powers at the disposal of the government on the other make nonsense of any idea that revolution could have been stopped if enough people had wanted it and gone about it in an efficient manner. That revolution did not occur in the period 1789–1848 must be attributed primarily to the absence of any popular desire for revolution.

If revolutionary endeavours were badly organised and badly supported it is not surprising that they never produced a winning strategy, but it must remain one of the most speculative aspects of the revolutionary movement in Great Britain whether anyone did in fact hit upon a scheme that might have worked had other circumstances been favourable. In the view of Asa Briggs, only a few had given serious thought, and this ineffective thought, to the problems of waging a revolution; [s3, *302*] and it will always remain open to debate whether a revolutionary coup in the capital and the assertion of power from the centre outwards was a more realistic notion than that of provincial movements which would coalesce in London, whether Spa Fields or Cato Street was inherently a better idea than Pentrich. Variations on these themes seem to have been few and limited. The notion of simultaneous mass meetings in 1819 seems to have occurred to a few as the means by which the masses might be mobilised at the same time throughout the country, and leadership given to them for rebellious purposes. Again in 1839 and 1848 mass meetings were thought by some as a possible route to insurrection, though the mechanics of such an operation have always been thoroughly obscure. Another, almost equally obscure, notion was that of revolution by means of general strike, which was first implemented in 1820 and repeatedly talked of during Chartism. This, in retrospect, seems the most promising plan for involving the mass of the population, and it was with this purpose that the tactic was invoked in 1820 rather than for the more aggressive purpose of stopping the national economy. The Chartists were moving more towards an appreciation of the kind of power that the workers as such had at their disposal if it could be mobilised, but in their own time it could not. There was neither the trade union organisation in support, nor even in existence, to make possible such a mobilisation, and such attempts as were made occurred when they were least likely to be a success. Successful industrial action through strikes required a position of economic strength for the strikers, to give them leverage. Had they possessed such economic strength, they would probably have been uninterested in exploiting it for political purposes; without it, the strikes of 1839 and 1842 must peter out and inflict more damage while they lasted on the strikers than on the employers and the government. The use of general strikes as a political weapon would require much more organisation and co-ordination between political and industrial movements than were possible by 1848, and the weapon has remained unused to this day.

The bigger question of the relationship between the course of the Industrial Revolution on the one hand and the revolutionary movement on the other is one that few contemporaries were able to consider in view of the relatively late appreciation of the nature of the industrial change that was taking place. The clarity of Marx's vision on the economic movement was not paralleled by an ability to predict its political consequences, and the belief that the emerging industrial proletariat would take revolutionary steps to acquire political power proved far wide of the mark. Whatever the precise course of average working-class living standards during the first half of the nineteenth century, there were sufficient improvements in the standards of the more skilled to detach them from the grievances of the unskilled and to give them a supposed vested interest in the perpetuation of that capitalist system which was to become increasingly cited as the appropriate target of revolutionary action from the working classes. And if the obvious beneficiaries of industrialisation were unlikely to step forward as revolutionaries, the obvious victims of it, the weavers, the framework-knitters, or the victims of technological redundancy such as the wool-combers and the croppers, were usually too caught up in the sheer struggle for survival to have the time and inclination for envisaging broader horizons. It is true that the industrial struggle did produce a new mass base in which radicalism could thrive, and it has been noted that the reform movements of

1815-19, compared with those of the 1790s, reflect a significant shift of emphasis from London and Edinburgh to Manchester and Glasgow. Yet the revolutionary storm-troopers, or even the most politically conscious, were not to be found among the factory workers, miners, and transport workers of the new industrial Britain. It was the small craftsmen – the cobblers, the hatters and the watchmakers; or the workshop- or home-based exponents of the hand-trades, the weavers or the stockingers, who were to be the political activists, while their brethren of the new and expanding industries turned to trade union organisation in so far as they interested themselves in mass working-class organisation. Of course, these generalisations, like all others, do not hold for every individual case, but they are sufficiently indicative of the overall position to suggest why hopes of revolution founded on the progress of the Industrial Revolution were not to be realised.

And part of the failure of the working classes to produce a unified response to industrialisation, whether in political terms such as by revolution, or in a trade union movement which incorporated unskilled as well as skilled workers, was the failure to produce a common ideology which could serve as a basis for such political or industrial action. In the 1790s, it has been argued, working men were much more inclined to form Church/King mobs and display their xenophobia in wild celebrations of victories over the enemy than they were to form revolutionary mobs. Popular sentiment, such as it was, was crudely patriotic and anti-French, and reform was identified with the foreign cause. Where riots occurred they concerned food, wages and unpopular recruiting methods, and there were even mutinies in the fleet and militia over conditions of service, but all these grievances were ends in themselves, not indicative of a common ideological position or able to be co-ordinated for protest against something bigger than the immediate target, the system of government, for instance, rather than a local baker. In Scotland there is some evidence of a greater political awareness, a greater concern for reform, and even the appearance of political slogans within bread-riots, and the west of Scotland rebels of 1820 also showed a greater political concern than their English counterparts of 1817. But this is insufficient to undermine the argument that the working classes failed to evolve a common ideological position for themselves as workers, that they continued to think in terms of race and religion rather than of class, and that their grievances remained immediate and able to be satisfied without the need for fundamental change within the social and political system. And when they had grievances they looked for their removal not to ideas by which a better system might be achieved but to leaders who might exploit the existing system to short-term advantage or, more likely, lead them up some blind alley according to the whims and fancies of the individual in command. William Lovett, in particular, called for ideas and not for leaders. [s33, *30*] The revolutionaries provided neither.

Ideas and leadership both in fact came from the very people who had felt themselves most threatened by working-class violence and working-class revolt during the first half of the nineteenth century, the governing classes. Their almost universal fear, which for a long time induced aggression, eventually gave rise to policies of appeasement, which successfully converted a feared enemy into a quiescent co-operator. Just as the landowners were able to assimilate the new industrial middle class into a power structure that remained basically intact through all the social changes that accompanied the Industrial Revolution, so did this new alliance become sufficiently sensitive and responsive to the needs of the new working classes that it was able to render these groups, if not satisfied, at least politically innocuous. Whatever the forces and motives responsible for the various reform movements of the 1830s and 1840s and the administrative and social changes that they initiated and implemented, the important fact is the willingness of parliament in these years to legislate where evil had been exposed and legislation was thought proper. Sanitary reform, the remedy of those who believed that urbanisation was the root of the working-class problem, had made little headway by the middle of the century, but those who believed that the industrial system itself was at fault had achieved notable successes in regulating working conditions, the Mines Act of 1844 and the Ten Hour Act of 1847. Working-class leaders and their humanitarian patrons from other social groups were convinced that many of the evils of urban working-class life, disease, drinking and domestic dislocation, for instance, derived from the long hours worked in factories, and the willingness of the legislature to intervene on behalf of the factory workers was a measure of reconciliation more important than the sanitary improvements that Chadwick offered. And if Parliament had no comparable offering for workers in the domestic trades, they were disappearing as a political problem by mid-century, as they were driven into alternative employment.

Education too was believed to be a powerful stabilising influence within society, for the educated worker, it was thought, would be a safer as well as a more useful member of the community. Despite the modest beginnings of government contributions to education in 1833, by the 1840s it was increasingly acknowledged by successive commissions of inquiry into different aspects of working-class life that the battle for men's minds was now on and that ignorant workers were a danger. As early as 1830 William Cobbett had attacked the Society for the Diffusion of Useful Knowledge as a confidence trick perpetrated upon the working classes to distract them from appreciating the real cause of their troubles and doing something to rectify their situation. [P59] And there is no doubt that the advocates of education were in part motivated by fear of the alternative if they failed to impose the ideas and values of the middle classes upon the workers and teach them the virtues that they ought to practise. It was one of the central lessons to be learned that working-class people should disavow politics, and the writing of an education clause into the 1833 Factory Act appropriately indicated the felt need to instruct the factory children as well as lighten their work-load.

If the diffusion of education would help to keep society free from revolution so too, it was believed, would the diffusion of religion, and of all religious groups the Methodists have traditionally been hailed as the saviours of Britain from revolution during these years when it appeared a possibility. The ambiguous role of Methodism as a force acting consecutively, even concurrently, for conservatism and for radicalism, has occasioned much debate, but few people would today suppose that the Methodists were sufficiently numerous or influential to have prevented revolution, even had their weight been cast firmly on one side of the argument. It would be a mistake to imagine, argues Hobsbawm, that the Methodists could have prevented revolution if other circumstances within Britain had been conducive to revolution in the late eighteenth or early nineteenth centuries, and few would be disposed to contest this judgment. There would be a similar readiness to share the view that Methodism achieved its stabilising social influence through the innumerable men who came up through the Sunday schools and chapels and took into industrial and political life the qualities and talents they had developed within Methodism and used them on behalf of the working classes in non-revolutionary ways. [s24, *33*; s40, *354–61*]

But more important than the externally imposed institutions, the schools and the chapels, in reconciling the working classes to industrialisation and drawing their political sting were their very own institutions, the trade unions, the friendly societies, the co-operative societies, and eventually the Labour Party, which were increasingly acceptable to employers and governments and safeguarded the position of working-class people within the industrial system. Machinery of protest became converted into machinery of acceptance, working within the system rather than seeking to overthrow it, and the working classes acquired a growing vested interest in the society that some of them had previously sought to overturn by violent revolution. And as they sought to promote their societies and organisations they became less fearful to the upper and middle classes, more trustworthy, able eventually to be entrusted with the vote, which the urban workers received in 1867, the vote which made them guardians of the state. So far had fear of revolution declined by this date.

Select Bibliography and Works Cited

PRIMARY SOURCES

I OFFICIAL PAPERS AND ARCHIVE MATERIAL

British Museum
P1 Place Collection, Add. MSS 27791-4

Derbyshire County Record Office
P2 Pentrich Collection

Glasgow City Archives
P3 Monteith Correspondence (1820), G 1/2

Kirkintilloch Burgh Council
P4 Peter Mackenzie Papers, NRA (Scot) 0347

National Library of Scotland
P5 Croker Correspondence (1820), MS 1819
P6 Court of Justiciary Trials, 1793-94 – Edinburgh, no date (*see also under* Scottish Record Office)
P7 Diary of C. H. Hutcheson, MS 2773
P8 Hardie (1820), MS 909
P9 Melville Correspondence (1792-1819), MS 6-1 (*see also under* Scottish Record Office)
P10 Sir Walter Scott Correspondence (1819-20), MS 3890-91

Nottingham City Archives
P11 Framework-Knitters' Papers, 1812-14
P12 Random Items

Nottingham University
P13 Newcastle MSS

Public Record Office
P14 Home Office Series 40, Correspondence etc. 1812-55, on Disturbances
P15 Home Office Series 41, Entry Books, 1816-98, on Disturbances
P16 Home Office Series 43, George III Correspondence, 1782-1820

P17   Home Office Series 44, George IV and later Correspondence, 1820–61
P18   Home Office Series 47, Expired Commissions, Judges' Reports, 1784–1829
P19   Privy Council Papers, Papers Relating to Corresponding Societies, PC i/41
P20   Treasury Solicitors' Papers, Series II

Scottish Record Office

P21   Court of Justiciary Processes, 1798 (*see also under* National Library of Scotland)
P22   Home Office Papers on Scotland (1816–21), RH 2/4, vols 111–37
P23   Melville Papers (1795–99), GD 51/5 (*see also under* National Library of Scotland)
P24   Papers Relating to William Skirving, RH 4/52

Stirling Burgh Library

P25   Correspondence relating to the execution of Baird and Hardie (1820)

II BOOKS, PAMPHLETS ETC.

P26   Aiton, R., *Inquiry into Present Distresses* etc. (Glasgow, 1820)
P27   Anonymous, *Trial for Libel . . . Richmond v. Simpkin and Marshall* etc. (Glasgow, pamphlet, undated [1834 or 1835])
P28   Bamford, S., *Passages in the Life of a Radical* (Manchester, 1838–41; repr. London, 1967)
P29   Burns, Robert, *Poetical Works*, ed. W. Wallace (Edinburgh and London, 1958)
P30   Cartwright, F. D., *Life and Works of Major Cartwright* (London, 1826)
P31   Cleland, J., *Rise and Progress of the City of Glasgow* (Glasgow, 1820)
P32   Cleland, J., *Enumeration of Glasgow* (Glasgow, 1820, 1831)
P33   Cockburn, Henry, *Journal*, vol. I (Edinburgh, 1874)
P34   Cockburn, Henry, *Sedition Trials* etc. (Edinburgh, 1888)
P35   Cockburn, Henry, *Memorials of His Time* (Edinburgh, 1856)
P36   Cooper, T., *Life of Thomas Cooper* (London, 1872)
P37   Felkin, W., *History of the Machine-wrought Hosiery and Lace Manufactures* (London, 1867; repr. Newton Abbot, 1967)
P38   Fyfe, J. G. (ed.), *Scottish Diaries and Memoirs, 1746–1843* (Stirling, 1942)
P39   Gammage, R. G., *History of the Chartist Movement* (London, 1854; Newcastle upon Tyne, 1894)
P40   'Gavroche', *Selections from the Writings of William Stewart* (Glasgow, 1948)
P41   *Glasgow Directory* (Glasgow, edns of 1816, 1818, 1822–3)
P42   Green, C. J., *Trials for High Treason in Scotland* etc. (Edinburgh, 1825)
P43   Hardie, A., *The Radical Revolt* etc. (Rutherglen, pamphlet, undated)
P44   Howell's *State Trials* (London, 1809–26)
P45   Lamond, R., *Narrative of . . . Emigration from . . . Lanark and Renfrew to Upper Canada* (Glasgow, 1821)

P46 Linton, W. J., *James Watson: A Memoir* (Manchester, 1880)
P47 Lovett, W., *Life and Struggles of William Lovett* (London, 1876; repr. 1920)
P48 Mackenzie, P., *Exposure of the Spy System . . . in Glasgow . . . 1816–1820* (Glasgow, 1833)
P49 McEwan, R. D., *Old Glasgow Weavers, 1514–1905* (Glasgow, 1908)
P50 Muir, J., *Account of the Execution of James Wilson* (broadsheet, undated, probably Glasgow, *c.* 1820)
P51 Paine, Thomas, *Rights of Man* (1791–2; repr. New York, 1969)
P52 Parkhill, John, *History of Paisley* (Paisley, 1857)
P53 Parkhill, John, *The Life and Opinions of Arthur Sneddon: An Autobiography* (Paisley, 1860)
P54 *Proceedings of the Society of United Irishmen of Dublin* (Dublin, 1793)
P55 Richmond, A. B., *Narrative of the Condition of the Manufacturing Population* etc. (Glasgow, 1825)
P56 Somerville, A., *The Autobiography of a Working Man* (London, 1848; repr. London, 1967)
P57 Wilde, John, *An Address to the Lately Formed Society of the Friends of the People* (Edinburgh, 1793)

III Periodicals

P58 *Annual Register*
P59 Cobbett's *Weekly Political Register*
P60 *Edinburgh Weekly Journal*
P61 *Glasgow Courier*
P62 *Glasgow Herald*
P63 Hansard's *Parliamentary Debates*
P64 *Leeds Mercury*
P65 *Northern Star*
P66 *Nottingham Journal*
P67 *Nottingham Review*
P68 *Scots Magazine*
P69 *Scotsman*
P70 *Spirit of the Union*
P71 *Stirling Journal*
P72 *The Times*

SECONDARY SOURCES

Works specially recommended for general study are indicated by an asterisk (*)

s1 Altick, R. D., *The English Common Reader, 1800–1900* (Chicago, 1957; repr. 1963)
s2 Blair, M., *The Paisley Shawl* (Paisley, 1904)
*s3 Briggs, A. (ed.), *Chartist Studies* (London, 1959; 1967 edn)
s4 Briggs, A., *The Age of Improvement* (London, 1959)
s5 Brinton, C., *A Decade of Revolution, 1789–99* (New York, 1934)
*s6 Brock, M., *The Great Reform Act* (London, 1973)
s7 Brown, P. A., *The French Revolution in English History* (London, 1918; repr. Liverpool, 1965)
*s8 Butler, J. R. M., *The Passing of the Great Reform Act* (London, 1914; 1964 edn)

s9   Chalmers, A. K., *Health of Glasgow, 1818–1925* (Glasgow, 1930)
s10   Chandler, F. W., *Political Spies and Provocative Agents* (Sheffield, 1933; 1936 edn)
s11   Cobban, A., *The Debate on the French Revolution, 1789–1800* (London, 1950)
s12   Cole, G. D. H., *Short History of the British Working Class Movement, 1789–1927* (London, 1927; 1948 edn)
s13   Cole, G. D. H. and Filson, A. W. (eds), *British Working Class Movements: Select Documents, 1789–1875* (London, 1951; 1965 edn)
s14   Cole, G. D. H. and Postgate, R. W., *The Common People* (London, 1938; 1946 edn)
s15   Crump, W. B., *The Leeds Woollen Industry, 1780–1830* (Leeds, 1931)
*s16 Darvall, F. O., *Popular Disturbance and Public Order in Regency England* (London, 1934)
s17   *Dictionary of National Biography* (Oxford, 1967–8 edn, vols 13 and 15)
s18   Drysdale, W., *Auld Biggins of Stirling* (Stirling, 1904)
s19   Ellis, P. B. and Mac A'Ghobhainn, S., *The Scottish Insurrection of 1820* (London, 1970)
s20   Groves, R., *But We Shall Rise Again: A History of Chartism* (London, 1938)
s21   Hamburger, J., *James Mill and the Art of Revolution* (New Haven, Conn., 1963)
s22   Hammond, J. L. and Hammond, B., *The Town Labourer, 1760–1832* (London, 1917)
s23   Hammond, J. L. and Hammond, B., *The Skilled Labourer* (London, 1919)
s24   Hobsbawm, E. J., *Labouring Men* (London, 1964; 1968 edn)
s25   Hobsbawm, E. J., *Industry and Empire* (London, 1968)
s26   Hovell, M., *The Chartist Movement* (Manchester, 1918; 1966 edn)
s27   Johnston, T., *The History of the Working Classes in Scotland* (Glasgow, 1922; Glasgow, 1946 edn)
s28   Kinsey, W., 'Some Aspects of Lancashire Radicalism' (M.A. thesis, Manchester University, 1927)
s29   MacPhail, I. M. M., *A Short History of Dunbartonshire* (Dumbarton, 1962)
s30   Maehl, W. H., *The Reform Bill of 1832: Why Not Revolution?* (London and New York, 1967)
s31   Manwaring, G. E. and Dobrée, B., *The Floating Republic* (London, 1937)
s32   Mather, F. C., *Public Order in the Age of the Chartists* (London, 1959)
s33   Mather, F. C., *Chartism* (London, 1968)
s34   Mathieson, W. L., *The Awakening of Scotland, 1747–97* (Glasgow, 1910)
s35   Meikle, H., *Scotland and the French Revolution* (Glasgow, 1912; repr. Liverpool, 1969)
s36   Neal, J., *The Pentrich Revolution* (Ripley, 1898; 1966 edn)
s37   Nimmo, W., *The History of Stirlingshire* (Hamilton, 1880)
s38   Pakenham, T., *The Year of Liberty* (London, 1969)
s39   Peel, F., *The Risings of the Luddites* (Heckmondwike, 1880)
s40   Perkin, H. J., *Origins of Modern English Society* (London, 1969)

s41 Prebble, J., *The Highland Clearances* (London, 1963; 1969 edn)
*s42 Read, D., *Peterloo: The 'Massacre' and its Background* (Manchester, 1958)
s43 Read, D. and Glasgow, E., *Feargus O'Connor, Irishman and Chartist* (London, 1961)
s44 Ridley, F. A., *The Revolutionary Tradition in England* (London, 1948)
s45 Roach, W. M., 'Radical Reform Movements in Scotland from 1815 to 1822' (Ph.D. thesis, Glasgow University, 1970)
s46 Rose, R., *Governing Without Consensus* (London, 1971)
s47 Rudé, G. F. E., *The Crowd in History, 1730–1848* (New York, 1964)
s48 Saunders, L. J., *Scottish Democracy, 1815–40* (Edinburgh, 1950)
s49 Saville, J., *Ernest Jones, Chartist* (London, 1952)
s50 Schoyen, A. R., *The Chartist Challenge* (London, 1958)
s51 Smelser, N. J., *Social Change in the Industrial Revolution* (London and Chicago, 1959)
s52 Smout, T. C., *A History of the Scottish People, 1560–1830* (London, 1969; 1972 edn)
s53 Tennant, C., *The Radical Laird* (Kineton–Warwick, 1970)
s54 Thomis, M. I., *Politics and Society in Nottingham, 1785–1835* (Oxford, 1969)
*s55 Thomis, M. I., *The Luddites* (Newton Abbot, 1970)
s56 Thompson, D., *The Early Chartists* (London, 1971)
*s57 Thompson, E. P., *The Making of the English Working Class* (London, 1968 edn)
s58 Trevelyan, G. M., *British History in the Nineteenth Century* (London, 1922; 1937 edn)
s59 Wallas, G., *The Life of Francis Place* (London, 1898)
s60 Walmsley, R., *Peterloo: The Case Reopened* (Manchester, 1969)
s61 Ward, J. T. (ed.), *Popular Movements, c. 1830–50* (London, 1970; repr. 1976)
*s62 Ward, J. T., *Chartism* (London, 1973)
s63 Webb, R. K., *The British Working Class Reader, 1790–1848* (London, 1955)
s64 West, J., *A History of the Chartist Movement* (London, 1920)
s65 White, R. J., *From Waterloo to Peterloo* (London, 1957; 1963 edn)
*s66 Williams, D., *John Frost: A Study in Chartism* (Cardiff, 1939)
*s67 Williams, G. A., *Artisans and Sans Culottes* (London, 1968)
s68 Wilson, A., *The Chartist Movement in Scotland* (Manchester, 1970)
s69 Young, D., *Edinburgh in the Age of Sir Walter Scott* (Norman, University of Oklahoma Press, 1965)

Index

Aberdeen 24, 31
Airdrie 81
Alloa 38
American Revolution 1, 6, 123
Anti-Corn-Law League, see Popular Movements
Apprenticeship Acts, Repeal of, 1813–14 30
aristocrats 5
arms, see Revolutionary Movement
Armstrong, J. 73
Arnold 45
artisans 8–9, 18, 27, 29, 70, 123
Attwood, T. 88–91, 94, 97, 118
Ayr 19
Ayrshire 19, 77, 81, 121

Bacon, J. and T., see Revolutionary Movement
Baines, J. 55
Baird, J., see Revolutionary Movement
Baker, R. 33
Balfron 75
Bamford, S. 37, 39, 43–4, 56, 58, 70, 104, 109
Basford 45
Baxter, J. 7
Beeston 87
Belfast 18, 31
Benbow, T. 88, 90, 103
Bennet, H. G. 120, 122
Bideford 37
Biggar, G. 41
Binns, B. 20
Binns, J. 20
Birmingham 23, 63, 88–90, 92, 94, 96–9, 101, 104, 106, 110
Black Lamp, see Revolutionary Movement
Blandford 88

Blanketeers, see Parliamentary Reform Movement
Bolton 31
Bonnymuir, Battle of, see Revolutionary Movement
Borders 72
Boswell, Col. A. 81
Bradford 45, 106, 109–10
Bradford, Maj.-General 69
Bradley the Spy 46, 58
Brandreth, J., see Revolutionary Movement
Braxfield, Lord 13
Brayshaw, J., see Revolutionary Movement
Bridport 37
Briggs, A. 111, 128
Bristol 87–8, 93, 95, 98
British Convention, see Parliamentary Reform Movement
Bulwell 45, 48
Burdett, Sir F. 36, 38, 46, 78, 125
Butterley 45, 50–1, 53–5
Byng, Maj.-General 44, 120

Camelon 75–6
Carlisle 31, 72, 125
Carmarthen 102
Carron Co. 75
Cartwright, J. 7, 11, 36–9
Castle, J. 41, 67
Castlereagh, Viscount 80
Cato Street Conspiracy, see Revolutionary Movement
Chadwick, E. 131
Chalmers, T. 77
Chartism, see Parliamentary Reform Movement
Cheshire 30
Chesterfield 50

Church/King riots, *see* Popular Movements
Cleary, T. 38
Cobbett, W. 7, 36, 38–9, 42, 46, 52, 54, 56–8, 91, 97, 123, 125, 132
cobblers 130
Cochrane, Lord 36, 39
Cockburn, H. 23, 26, 69, 80, 88, 127
Coldham, G. 33
colliers 74, 77
Colwick Hall 87
Combination Laws, 1799–1800 16, 30, 82
Conant, N. 33
Condorrat 76
conspiracies, *see* Revolutionary Movement
Cook, T. 76
Cooper, T. 107, 109
Co-operative Societies 132
Cope, J., *see* Revolutionary Movement
Corresponding Societies, *see* Parliamentary Reform Movement
Corresponding Societies Act, 1799 16
cotton manufacturers 30
cotton spinners 72, 74, 77
cotton weaving 63, 121
Craig, R. 73
Craigdallie, J. 19
Crawford, S. 101
croppers 32, 119, 129
Cross, Lawyer 120
Cupar 19

Daer, Lord 8
Darvall, F. O. 117
de Tocqueville 118
Declaration of Arbroath 5
Denman, T. 49, 58, 120
Derby 29, 43, 60–1, 82, 87
Derbyshire 31, 36, 43, 47, 51–2, 55, 74
Despard, E. 22, 29, 36
Devonshire, Duke of 52
Dewsbury 109
Dissenters 23
Dog and Partridge, Middleton 56
Downie, D. 17–18
Dublin 10, 20, 31
Dumfermline 19
Dumfriesshire 72
Dunbartonshire 75, 77
Dundas, H. 24
Dundee 8–9, 19, 24, 37–8, 71–2
Duntocher 75

East Anglia 37
East Lothian 25
East Midlands 31–4, 37, 45, 70, 120
East of Scotland 71
Eastwood 51–2
Edinburgh 8–10, 12–14, 17–19, 24, 27, 38, 72, 76, 79, 80, 82, 129
education 131–2
election riots, *see* Popular Movements
Enfield, H. 47, 54, 56
Erskine, H. 14
Exeter 54

factories 32, 34, 77
factory reform 93, 119, 132
factory workers 21, 77, 106, 119, 130–2
Fairly, J. 18
Falkirk 75
Fife 19
Finlay, K. 30, 41
Fitzwilliam, Earl 33
Fletcher, A. 14
food prices 120
food riots, *see* Popular Movements
Forfarshire 19
Fox, C. J. 9
framework-knitters 27, 29, 31–2, 37, 55, 119, 129
France 11
Fraser, J. 82
French Revolution 1, 2, 6, 9, 21, 27, 36, 112, 117–18, 122–3
Friendly Societies 132
Friends of Liberty, *see* Parliamentary Reform Movement
Friends of the People, *see* Parliamentary Reform Movement
Frost, J. 104–5, 109–10, 113, 115–16
Fulton, R. 73

Gammage, R. G. 106
gentry 8
Germiston 75
Gerrald, J. 5, 9–10
Glasgow 8, 10, 18–19, 27, 30–2, 37–41, 63, 65, 67, 69–82, 121–2, 125, 130
  Earl of 68
  Herald 79
  University 14
Glorious Revolution 5
Gloucester 98
Gordon Riots, *see* Popular Movements
Graham, Sir J. 114
Greenock 76

Greville 112
Grey, Lord 9, 41, 86–7, 89–90, 92–3, 97

Habeas Corpus Act 13, 15, 40, 42–3,
    62, 124
Halifax 55
Hamilton 66
Hamilton, R. 73
Hammond, J. L. and B. 52
Hampden, J. 5, 123
Hampden Clubs, see Parliamentary
    Reform Movement
handloom weavers, see weavers
Hardie, A., see Revolutionary Movement
Hardy, T. 10–12, 14–15, 23
Harney, J. 103–4, 107–8, 112, 115
hatters 130
Henson, G. 31–3
Hertfordshire Yeomanry 99
Hetherington, H. 110
Highlands 72, 79
Hobhouse, J. C. 92
Hobsbawm, E. J. 117–18, 132
Hopkirk, T. 73
Horsfall, W. 36
hosiery 31, 48, 120
Hucknall 45
Huddersfield 33, 44, 47
Hume, J. 79–80, 98
Hunt, H. 36, 39, 64
Huskisson, W. 82
Hutchison, J. 73

Industrial Revolution, social and poli-
    tical consequences 3, 8, 27, 67,
    118, 122, 129–31
Ireland 11
Irish 21–2, 78, 121
Irish Confederates 109
iron-founders 74

Jacobins 5, 8, 16, 21–3, 27, 36, 45,
    55
Jeffrey, F. 82, 95
Jones, E. 102

Kennington Common 106, 109
Kilbarchan 75
Kilsyth 74, 76, 80
Kimberley 45
King, J., see Revolutionary Movement
Kinloch, G. 71
Kirkcaldy 10
Kirkintilloch 18, 75

Labour Party 132
labourers' riots, see Popular Movements
Lanark 24
Lanarkshire 41, 73
Lancashire 20, 22, 30, 32–5, 38, 41, 44,
    47, 56, 61, 64–5, 70, 73, 75, 79, 104,
    115, 119
Leeds 63, 110
Leeds Mercury 60
Leicester 47, 56, 101, 103
Leicestershire 31
Liverpool 30, 44
Llanidloes 106
Locke, J. 7
Lockhart, J. G. 81
London 15, 18, 26, 29, 33, 39–42, 44–9,
    56, 60, 63, 65–7, 70, 73, 81, 90–2, 94,
    97–9, 109, 110, 112–13, 128, 130
London Corresponding Society, see
    Parliamentary Reform Movement
London Whig Club 15
Loughborough 47, 113
Lovett, W. 101–2, 107, 131
Luddism, see Popular Movements
Ludlam, I., see Revolutionary Move-
    ment: Pentrich Rebellion
Lyon, Maj.-General 43, 120

McCracken, H. J. 21
McDouall, P. 107
machine-makers 74
McIntyre, J. 71
Mackintosh, J. 6
McLauchlin, J. 41
Magna Carta 5
Maitland, General 40
Manchester 21, 23, 34, 38, 42, 45, 56,
    63–5, 69, 71, 73, 75, 79, 106, 108,
    110, 114, 125, 130
    Gazette 65
    Guardian 92
Margarot, M. 10
Markham, J. 103
Marx, K. 129
Mealmaker, G. 19–20
Melbourne, Lord 89
Mellor, G. 36
Merthyr Tydfil 37
Methodism 27, 32, 63, 132
Middle Classes and Reform 38, 87, 89,
    97, 102, 108, 115
    and Revolution 87, 90–7, 116–19,
    128
    class consciousness 113

Middle Classes and Reform (*cont.*)
  in power 131
  values 132
Middleton 34, 37, 56
Middleton, Lord 53
Millar, J. C. 14
miners 105–6, 130
Mines Act, 1844 131
Mitchell, J. 44, 70
Monmouth 104, 110–11
Monmouthshire 100, 104, 109
Muir, T. 5, 9–12, 15, 18–20
Municipal Corporations' Act, 1835 98

nailers 119
Napier, Colonel 90, 112–15
National Union of Working Classes, *see*
  Parliamentary Reform Movement
Nationalism 10–11, 18–19, 21–2
naval mutinies, *see* Popular Move-
  ments
Newark 47
Newcastle upon Tyne 37, 104, 110
Newcastle, Duke of 42, 51–3, 61, 87–8,
  120
Newport 100, 105, 109–11, 113, 116
Newspaper Act, 1798 16
Nonconformists 23
Nore 25–6
Northern Star 107
Norwich 8
Nottingham 8, 23, 31–3, 37, 42–53, 56,
  58–9, 87–9, 112, 120, 125
Nottinghamshire 31, 33, 44, 50–1, 74,
  127
Nottingham Journal 54
Nottingham Political Union 89

oaths, *see* Revolutionary Movement
O'Brien, B. 102, 104, 144
O'Connor, F. 103, 107–9, 114
Oliver the Spy, *see* Revolutionary Move-
  ment

Page, J., *see* Revolutionary Movement
Paine, T. 6, 8–9, 15, 55, 97
Paineites 6
Paisley 18, 23, 37, 66, 68, 72–4, 76, 82,
  125
Palmer, Rev. T. 9–10, 15, 19
Parkes, J. 89–91, 94, 98
Parkhead 73, 80
Parkhill, J., *see* Revolutionary Move-
  ment

Parliamentary Reform Movement
  extent of popular support 7–8, 13,
    24–7 29, 32, 36–9, 62–5, 85,
    124, 129–30
  government attitude to 2–3, 7, 9–17,
    22–3, 27, 29, 35, 38, 40–4, 61–9,
    82–5, 123–4, 127
  ideology 5–8, 10, 13, 18–19, 39, 64
  methods 6, 9–12, 15–17, 19, 27, 39,
    43, 63–6
  origins 1–3
  progress of 8–9, 15, 23, 26–7, 36–9,
    62–4, 85, 129–30
  revolutionary implications 6, 7, 9,
    11–13, 123–4
  social composition 8, 27, 29, 36–8
  —particular groups
  Blanketeers 42
  British Convention 5–6, 8–13, 15,
    17–19
  Chartism 100–16
    aims 100
    arming 102–5
    contrast with middle-class threat
      116
    degree of popular support 100–1
    demonstrations 104–6
    difficulties of interpretation 11, 101
    general strike 74, 104, 106–8, 112,
      128–9
    government strength 112–14
    moral and physical force 82, 101–3
    Newport Rising 100, 105, 109–10
    organisational weaknesses 115–16
    popular support for 100, 114–15
    possible revolutionary strategies
      111–12
    rebellions 105–6, 108–11, 127
    riots 101, 106
    social composition 100
    threat of revolution 3, 97, 100–16
  Friends of Liberty 9, 19
  Friends of the People 8
  Hampden Clubs 36, 38–9, 41–5,
    55–6, 62, 70, 124, 126
  London Corresponding Society 5,
    7–12, 15–16, 20, 123–4, 126
  Peterloo 63–6, 68–9, 104
  Scottish Friends of the People 8–10,
    14, 17–18, 20, 24, 78
  Society for the Promotion of Con-
    stitutional Information 7, 15
  Union Societies 63, 66, 69, 71, 78–9, 81
  Yorkshire Movement 11

Parliamentary Reform Movement (*cont.*)
 The Reform Bill Crisis 85–99
  arming 89–91
  government strength 98–9
  loyalty of army 98–9
  National Union of Working Classes 89–90, 93–5, 126
  political unions 81, 87–90, 93, 96–9
  probability of revolution 94–8
  Reform Bill riots 86–8, 93, 95–6, 98–9
  revolution as a threat 83–6, 89–99
  role of extra-parliamentary pressure 96–7
  role of working classes 93–5
  strategy of revolution 91–3
Peasants' Revolt 118
Peel, Sir R. 82, 96
Pentrich 45–7, 50, 53, 55–7, 59, 82, 124–5
Pentrich Rebellion, *see* Revolutionary Movement
Perth 18–19, 24
Perthshire 19, 25
Peterloo, *see* Parliamentary Reform Movement
Pitt, W. 13, 15–16, 36
Place, F. 36, 90–1, 93–9, 102, 108
Plug Plot 106–7, 115
political unions, *see* Parliamentary Reform Movement
Pollockshaws 69
Pontefract 120
Poor Law 77
Poor Man's Guardian 95
Popular Movements
—general 2–3, 29, 37–8, 62, 83, 85, 100, 126–7
—particular
  Anti-Corn-Law League 85
  Church/King riots 2, 9, 12, 23–4, 130
  food riots 3, 13, 16, 24–6, 28–9, 31, 34, 37, 83, 127, 130
  Gordon Riots 2, 34
  labourers' riots 83, 87
  Luddism 3, 30, 32–7, 40, 51, 54, 58, 91, 117, 127–8
  militia riots 3, 20, 24–5, 28, 31, 130
  naval mutinies 3, 13, 24–6, 28, 128, 130
  political riots 24–5
  Society for Parliamentary Relief 31
  strikes 13, 30–2, 48, 62, 71–5, 94, 100, 104, 106–8, 112, 122, 128–9

trade unionism 30–4, 85, 93, 129–30, 132
Porter, J. 72, 125
Preston 31, 37
Price, Dr R. 7
prices 33, 120, 122
Protestants 18, 21

Quigley, Father 20

Ramsden, J. 33
religion 79, 132
Renfrewshire 75–6
republicanism 10–11, 18, 21, 97
Revolutionary Movement
 general
  arms 12, 18, 22, 28, 35, 48, 53–4, 64–5, 103–4
  causes of 118–24
  conspiracies 2–3, 12–13, 15–23, 28, 33, 35, 39, 41–4, 56–8, 64–6, 68–70, 82–3, 100, 124, 127
  declining fear of 132–3
  extent of popular support 2, 11, 18–24, 28–9, 70–1, 126–30
  government strength 127–8
  oath-taking 19, 22, 41, 67, 70
  origins 1–2, 11, 17, 19–20, 28, 35, 42–4, 62, 64–71, 122
  revolutionary situations 86–7, 93, 117–20, 122
  role of Methodism 132
  role of social reform 131–2
  social composition 119
  spies 40–1, 43–8, 53–4, 56, 61–2, 67–70, 109, 126–8
  strategy 128–9
  strength of threat 124–30
  weakness of organisation 28, 125–7
 Black Lamp 22
 Cato Street Conspiracy 41, 47, 65, 73, 128
 Pentrich Rebellion, 1817 43–62, 67, 82, 89, 120–1, 128
  aims 48–9
  Bacon, J. 49, 56
  Bacon, T. 45–9, 55–8, 61, 120, 125
  Brandreth, J. 29, 46–8, 50–1, 54–5, 59–61, 82, 120
  Cope, J. 53
  events 50–1
  government instigation 57–60
  government preparations 47, 49
  leadership 54–7

Revolutionary Movement (*cont.*)
  Pentrich Rebellion (*cont.*)
    Ludlam, I. 50, 55, 60–1
    nature of arms 53
    Oliver the Spy 43–51, 56–60, 67, 70, 120, 125
    origins 43–5, 120–1
    Page, J. 49
    preparations 44–6
    social composition 54–5, 124
    strategy of rebellion 47–8, 124
    support for 51–3, 124
    trials for prisoners 60–1
    Turner, W. 52, 55, 60–1
  Spa Fields 39, 41, 65, 67, 128
  Spenceans 41, 67
  United Englishmen 16, 18, 20–2, 25
  United Irishmen 10–11, 16, 18–22, 128
  United Scotsmen 16, 18–22, 25, 128
  West of Scotland Rebellion, 1820
    aims 78–9
    Armstrong, J. 73
    Baird, J. 76–8, 82
    Battle of Bonnymuir 76–9, 81
    Brayshaw, J. 63, 73, 78–9
    Craig, R. 73
    degree of support 72, 74–7, 81–2, 124
    events 73–7
    Fulton, R. 73
    Hardie, A. 66, 76–7, 79, 82, 121–2
    Hutchison, J. 73
    King, J. 81
    leaders 78–9, 125
    McIntyre, J. 71
    organisation 71–5, 81, 125
    origins 71–2, 121-2
    Parkhill, J. 73
    Porter, J. 72, 125
    preparedness of authorities 74, 80–1
    results 81–2
    Richmond, A. 41, 67–70, 80
    role of informers 72, 79–81
    Scottish nationalism 78–9
    Smith, W. 72, 125
    social composition of rebels 77–8, 124
    strategy 71, 73–4, 76, 124
    Strathaven Rising 75–7, 80–1, 122
    Wilson, J. 75, 77–8, 82
  Rights of Man 15

riots, *see* Popular Movements
Roebuck, J. A. 97
Rolleston, L. 51–2, 60, 89
Roman Catholics 18, 82
Rostow, W. W. 118
Rutherglen 65
Ryder, R. 40
Rye 87

St Peter's Fields 42, 63
sanitary reform 131
Scots Greys 99
Scott, Sir W. 81
Scottish Friends of the People, *see* Parliamentary Reform Movement
Scottish Nationalism 78–9
Sedition and Treason Bills 1795 14, 16
Seditious Meetings Act, 1817 40, 62
Sharp, T. 73
Sheffield 8, 15, 18, 22, 45–6, 50, 57, 90, 109, 125
Shelbourne, Lord 16
Sherborne 88
shoemakers 77
Sidmouth, Lord 40, 42, 44, 50, 57–8, 67, 69, 71
Six Acts, 1819 65, 69–70
Skirving, W. 10, 12–13
Sketchley, J. 101
Smith, A. 45, 53
Smith, W. 72, 125
smiths 77
Society for the Diffusion of Useful Knowledge 132
Society for Parliamentary Relief, *see* Popular Movements
Society for the Promotion of Constitutional Information, *see* Parliamentary Reform Movement
Somerville, A. 99, 113
South Wales 104, 109–10, 115
South Wingfield 45, 49–50
Spa Fields, *see* Revolutionary Movement
Spenceans, *see* Revolutionary Movement
spies, *see* Revolutionary Movement
Spithead 25
Staffordshire 105–6
Stephens, Rev. J. R. 103
Stevens, W. 43–4, 51
Stirling 18, 38, 81
Stirlingshire 75–7
stockingers, *see* framework-knitters
Stockport 34, 63
Stone 105

Strathaven 73, 76, 78, 80, 82
strikes, *see* Popular Movements
Sutton-in-Ashfield 54
Swanwick 46

tailors 77
Tayside 19
Ten-Hour Act, 1847 131
Thistlewood, A. 65
Thrushgrove 39
Times, The 98
Tiverton 88
Tone, W. 18, 21
trade unions, *see* Popular Movements
Tranent 25
transport workers 130
Trent, river 47
Trowbridge 104
Turner, J. 82
Turner, W., *see* Revolutionary Movement

Union Societies, *see* Parliamentary Reform Movement
Unitarians 9
United Englishmen, *see* Revolutionary Movement
United Irishmen, *see* Revolutionary Movement
United Scotsmen, *see* Revolutionary Movement
Unlawful Oaths' Act, 1797 16
urbanisation 67, 131

Vincent, H. 103, 105, 111

wages 27, 30–1, 33, 37, 62, 120–2
Wakefield 44–5, 48–9, 56, 58–9
Wallas, G. 90, 94, 114
Walsall 37

watchmakers 130
Watt, R. 17–18
weavers 11, 15, 27, 30–2, 37, 63, 65, 72–8, 119, 121–2, 129–30
Weightman, G. 50–1, 55, 60–1
Wellington, Duke of 87, 89–97, 113
West of Scotland 30, 63, 65, 71, 74, 77, 79, 130
West Riding 20–2, 32–3, 44, 57, 70, 106, 114–15
Western Vindicator 110
Westhoughton 34, 68
Westminster 36
Wetherall, Sir Chas. 88
White Horse Inn, Pentrich 50, 61
Wilford 54
Wilson, J., *see* Revolutionary Movement
Wiltshire 104
Windham, W. 13
Wollaton 46, 53
woolcombers 119, 129
woollen workers 32
working classes
  and Chartism 100, 102, 104–5, 116
  and reform 8–9, 27, 36–9, 62, 93–4, 123
  and revolution 2–3, 34, 52, 64–5, 71, 81, 87, 89–90, 93–5, 99, 103, 111–12, 116, 118, 129–30
  political consciousness 116, 119, 127, 130
  social grievances 22–3
  standard of living 129
  assimilation 131–3
wrights 74
Wyvill, C. 11, 16

Yeovil 88
Yorkshire 22, 32–6, 38, 47, 56, 61, 104, 106, 115